The E-Privacy
Imperative

The E-Privacy Imperative

Protect Your Customers' Internet Privacy
and Ensure Your Company's Survival in
the Electronic Age

Mark S. Merkow, CCP, CISSP

James Breithaupt

AMACOM

American Management Association

New York • Atlanta • Brussels • Buenos Aires • Chicago • London • Mexico City
San Francisco • Shanghai • Tokyo • Toronto • Washington, D.C.

Special discounts on bulk quantities of AMACOM books are available to corporations, professional associations, and other organizations. For details, contact Special Sales Department, AMACOM, a division of American Management Association, 1601 Broadway, New York, NY 10019.

Tel.: 212-903-8316. Fax: 212-903-8083.

Web site: www.amacombooks.org

This publication is designed to provide accurate and authoritative information in regard to the subject matter covered. It is sold with the understanding that the publisher is not engaged in rendering legal, accounting, or other professional service. If legal advice or other expert assistance is required, the services of a competent professional person should be sought.

Library of Congress Cataloging-in-Publication Data

Merkow, Mark S.
  The e-Privacy imperative : protect your customers' internet privacy and ensure your company's survival in the electronic age / Mark S. Merkow, James Breithaupt.
    p. cm.
  Includes bibliographical references and index.
  ISBN 0-8144-0628-9
    1. Electronic commerce. 2. Electronic commerce—Security measures. 3. Business enterprises—Computer networks—Security measures. 4. Privacy, Right of.   I. Breithaupt, Jim II. Title.

HF5548.32 .M47 2002
658.4′78—dc21

2001045906

Printing number
10 9 8 7 6 5 4 3 2 1

Contents

Acknowledgments

Of all the books that Jim and I have written together, this was—by far—the toughest one to wrestle to the ground. Seems that privacy is less a technology problem and more a people problem, and people are unpredictable. If you think of trying to solve a Rubik's Cube puzzle, but adding three more dimensions, you'll gain the right spin on the problem. To that end, it has been a long haul, and many people were needed to help complete the journey.

For starters, my friend and co-author, Jim Briethaupt, has been an absolute trooper, a loyal ally, and an outstanding collaborator in ferreting out the truth from the fiction in the endless paper mill about privacy. Thanks Jim for your dedication, hard work, artful muse, and insightful thinking that's made this book possible in the first place.

Thanks to my wife, Amy Merkow, as always, for her positive attitude and undying encouragement to keeping me with pen in hand.

The following people deserve gratitude beyond measure for their help, support, encouragement, and reassurance that's always needed to prevent authors from bagging a project: David Armes, Michael Barrett, Toby Barrick, Pete Bennett, Bill Blaney, Fred Bishop, Dr. James Dzierzanowski, Gleda Edwards, Allen Forbes, Roger Fox, Stephen Gibbons, Mark Griffith, Bill Hohle, Troy Hollis, Michael Kibbe, Don Kuecker, Joe Lesko, Sally Meglathery, John McDonald, Jonalyn McLeod, Jeff Palmeri, Harry Pearson, Angela Poletis, and Danny Yong.

To our kids, Josh Merkow, Jasmine Merkow, Brandon Bohlman, and Caitlyn Bohlman for their courage and support throughout the seemingly endless book creation process.

Tremendous thanks goes to Jacquie Flynn of AMACOM for all her help and support in turning a lump of clay into a finished product. Thanks are also in order to Rob Emenecker for his commitment to excellence he's demonstrated throughout.

Special thanks goes to my agent, Carole McClendon at Waterside Production, for an amazing ability to keep good news coming along regularly!

Thanks also to a cast of countless people from organizations across the globe who've contributed time, material, or expertise toward producing this book: Ernst and Young, Amazon.com, Yahoo!, Netscape, American Express Corporation, Anonymizer.com, Arizona State University, Travelocity, TRUSTe, PrivacyBot, Websense, Spectorsoft, WinWhatWhere, Carfax.com, American Institute of Certified Public Accountants (AICPA), American Management Association, Direct Marketing Association, Pew Internet and American Life Project, Forrester Research, Federal Trade Commission, US Department of Justice, and the World Wide Web Consortium (W3C).

—Mark Merkow

More than any other issue, the privacy issue blurs the division between politics and technology. Without advances in technology, we wouldn't have the truly amazing and world-altering advances in our lives and societies brought to us by the Internet. However, such mach-speed developments have left many of us wondering about our private lives and how safe we are from the prying eyes of others. This quandary prompts me to acknowledge my father

George, now deceased, a small town lawyer in Ohio who understood more than anyone I ever met the roles of individuals and government in our society. He believed we should not let the tools our society has at its disposal become a means of widening the gulf between us. Our tools should unite us, not divide us, and should be used for the people and by the people, not against the people by our institutions. My mother, Martha Holmes, also deceased, defied technology and stuck with her painting and sculpture. She trusted only those things she was responsible for bringing into the world, such as her art, and children.

I must also thank my wife, Margaret, who permitted me one more exception to the rule of no more book writing, and to my daughter, Faye, and son, Bo, who are growing up in a world I would never have guessed or imagined twenty years ago. They will bear witness to the world we are building.

And now for the professional "mercis." To Jacquie Flynn, our editor at Amacom who dogged us with her queries and edits, as a good editor should. She believed in what turned out to be a highly quixotic and elusive topic for a book and never gave up on us. To my co-author, Mark Merkow, who once again gave me the opportunity to work with him on this book. I would also like to thank the following publishers and their authors for allowing us to quote from their works: to the MIT Press for their permission to quote Simon Davies from his article "Re-Engineering the Right to Privacy" in the book *Technology and Privacy: The New Landscape*, edited by Philip Agre and Marc Rotenberg; to the Brookings Institution for their permission to quote Peter Swire from his book, *None of Your Business*; and to Peter Swire himself for several conversations we had about the EU Directive and his role as Chief Counselor for Privacy in the United States Office of Management and Budget in the Clinton adminstration.

—Jim Breithaupt

PART 1

E-Privacy
Is a Business
Priority

Consumer Privacy

Is the Internet eroding what little is left of individual privacy? The truth is that with each click on some irresistible online offer, consumers may be giving up a little bit of themselves. They are often surprised and annoyed when they're consequently inundated with even better offers or added junk mail the next time they log on. When consumers vocalize their concerns, online businesses such as yours might find that they are scrambling to devise an online privacy policy or defend their policy should they have one.

Can you say with any certainty that your e-commerce services aren't a part of the problem?

The climate of today's Internet—where it's commonplace to sell electronic lists containing thousands or millions of unsuspecting e-mail users and to place invisible cookies on browsers so third parties can follow consumers from site to site, building profiles on their activities—has created potentially insurmountable problems that may, in time, doom the promises of e-commerce.

Customer Concerns

The media loves stories of Internet information abuses and goes out of its way to make sure that everyone knows about these stories. Daily reports of stolen credit card numbers, Trojan horse and virus attacks designed to steal users' files from their PCs, and respectable corporations that are suddenly caught with their pants down when an expert—or government agency—reveals shady practices (see sidebars about DoubleClick and Toysmart) only serve to heighten the fears and drive people away from a technology that otherwise benefits them. Rather than embrace the new medium, people are left with little choice but to distrust it and are demanding that something be done about security—even if that means that the government steps in.

An Electronic Privacy Information Center (EPIC) report, entitled "Surfer Beware: Personal Privacy and the Internet," offers an insightful look at specific consumer privacy concerns. These concerns, ranked in order, include:

- Collection of personal information

- Presence and adequacy of privacy policies

- Access to one's own data

- Anonymity

- The use of cookies (when, how, and why)

- Spam

Any privacy systems solution must address all of these concerns or it is useless: consumers won't feel protected.

Self-Reliance or Government Regulation?
A Question as Old as the Country

Before addressing these concerns, however, we need to understand that the privacy issue in this country is not a new concern. Americans have always coveted their privacy and worried about the encroachment of their government into personal matters. The advancement of technology has only heightened public concern about their privacy. An increasing reliance upon computers and the Internet, the explosive growth of e-commerce, and other electronic means of communication such as wireless phones have opened new doors into the private lives of consumers, thus taking the privacy issue out of the strictly political realm and moving it into the consumer realm as well.

In his article "Re-Engineering the Right to Privacy," the general director of Privacy International, Simon Davies, describes this phenomenon, the path privacy issues have followed "from the political realm to the consumer realm," a journey that has turned privacy into a commodity. Privacy policies have become a costly "add-on" that companies with an Internet presence must institute to survive.[1] Privacy is a commodity in the sense that it has value to the individual and the individual's personal data is being captured and sold on the Internet. Privacy is an "add-on" in that businesses must now consider security and privacy matters in their IT budget. According to Davies, this journey has been the triumph of "public interest" over the interests of government, less in terms of the gains that the individual has made in protecting personal information as forcing the issue of privacy into public debate.

1. Simon Davies, "Re-Engineering the Right to Privacy," in *Technology and Privacy: The New Landscape*, Philip E. Agre and Marc Rotenberg, Eds. (Cambridge, Mass.: MIT Press 1997).

Figure 1-1   A Privacy Timeline

1791	1876	1890	1928	1948
Congress ratifies Bill of Rights	Alexander Graham Bell raises question of who owns a conversation as he introduces the telephone	U.S. Census Bureau uses electro-mechanical punch card machine to tabulate its citizens	U.S. Supreme Court in *Olmstead v. U.S.* supports legality of wiretapping without a warrant	Claude Shannon of MIT writes about cryptographic theory and attracts attention of government

1965	1966	1967	1969	1970
U.S. Supreme Court upholds right to privacy in the matter of contraception	Congress passes the Freedom of Information Act	U.S. Supreme Court reverses its decision in the *Olmstead* case	ARPANET, DOD's forerunner of the Internet, comes online	Congress passes the Fair Credit Reporting Act

1974	1976	1977	1986	1987
Congress passes the Privacy Act guaranteeing access to government records	U.S. Supreme Court in *U.S. v. Miller* declares that individuals have no "expectation of privacy" in financial transactions	U.S. Privacy Protection Study Commission warns of growing threat to privacy	Congress passes the Electronic Communications Privacy Act	Robert Bork's failed Supreme Court nomination leads to the Video Privacy Protection Act

1990	1991	1993	1996	1997
A California court decides that employers may monitor employees' mail	Phil Zimmerman releases Pretty Good Privacy (PGP)	The first Web browser is released as public use of the Internet explodes	Number of identity thefts doubles since 1992 as E-commerce explodes	FTC requires marketers to obtain parental permission before marketing to children

1998	1999	1999	2000	2000
American Internet businesses face exclusion from Europe because of lax privacy standards	U.S. Ninth District Court rules that restrictions on export of strong key cryptography violate First Amendment	FTC reports in "Self-Regulation and Privacy Online" that few web sites follow basic information privacy practices	FTC releases report indicating industry's failure to self-regulate and recommending a set of fair information practices	Senator John McCain of AZ introduces Internet Privacy bill that would require web sites to reveal what they do with personal data

This debate over the right of the individual to protect his personal data is intricately tied to the political and social development of the United States, a debate that has intensified in the postindustrial age of high technology. Americans associate freedom with individuality and privacy. This country has continued to wrestle with legislation that profoundly affects our ability to protect personal information. And yet, at no other time in our history has our house been so besieged, and our right to privacy been in such jeopardy.

There has been an assault upon our individuality, a loss of identity, and a gradual erosion of our privacy. This long march toward what some privacy advocates would call a crisis in the right to privacy has not happened overnight. Figure 1-1 shows important dates in the political and technological development that have taken us to the age of the Internet.

The FTC and Online Privacy

Since 1995, the Federal Trade Commission (FTC) has been studying online privacy issues in an attempt to answer a fundamental question: can the online industry be trusted to self-regulate, or is government intervention required? The FTC's interest in the issue has grown as public awareness and concern over the way that online companies are collecting, storing, transferring, and analyzing their personal data has increased. The FTC recognizes that to ensure the continued growth of the online marketplace, they must allay consumer fears over loss of privacy and win their confidence. The question is, how active a role should the federal government, specifically the FTC, play in this twenty-first century drama?

Over the past several decades, the government has not exactly earned the confidence of its citizens in privacy matters. From the use of illegal wiretaps to keeping secret dossiers on political figures and average citizens, the government has a checkered past. This history of government intrusion into the lives of its citizens is amply documented in other works, and quite thoroughly in Simson

Garfinkel's excellent book, *Database Nation* (O'Reilly & Associates, 2000).

Privacy advocates continue to be alarmed by the U.S. government's policy toward national databases that link citizens' data across trackable activities (e.g., social security number activity) and national ID cards for access to government services (an idea abandoned in the mid-60s after public outcry); its desire to build network architectures that would allow them to listen in on private conversations and read e-mail; its reluctance to allow the export of strong cryptography tools for fear that criminals will "hide" their tracks and communications; and its promotion of the "Clipper Chip," which would have given the government the "secret code" to unlock any encrypted message it deemed critical to U.S. security interests. Some privacy advocates feel the U.S. government's involvement in online privacy regulation is akin to asking the fox to watch the hen house.

The conflict among interests of national security, consumer rights, and the individual's right to protect personal data such as medical and financial information has only been made more acute by the rapid movement of data and simplified tracking of it from its source to its destination within the explosive online economy. Along with an increased availability of information through electronic mediums has come an increased opportunity to use that information inappropriately or illegally. The Internet is now the backbone of most corporate networks and is becoming as popular as television and the radio in most households, driving people to increase their uses of it—often without regard for the potential abuses of personal information that we read about daily. In fact, the use of Internet devices in the home is blurring the once clear distinctions of networked and computerized devices versus noncomputerized devices.

A major problem that the federal government has faced when considering the regulation of the online economy is its inability to keep up with the frantic pace at which the technology continues to change. Recognizing this problem, the government has more or less chosen a *laissez-faire* attitude toward the Internet. It really had little choice. Before the ink would have a chance to dry on any piece of regulatory legislation, the technology will no doubt have redefined itself, rendering the government's efforts meaningless.

However, sensing growing consumer concern over privacy matters and the intrusion of online businesses on the Internet, the FTC continues to move in the direction of increased government involvement while noting the industry's inability to self-regulate. A quick rundown of news stories tells the tale of increasing government involvement:

• **June 1998.** The FTC tells Congress that the online industry had "fallen far short of what is needed to protect consumers," and promises a future study that will report on the progress that has been made.[2]

• **July 13, 1999.** While noting that businesses still have much work to do to protect the privacy of consumers online, the FTC recommended that Congress hold off on legislation that would regulate how companies collect and use consumer information.[3] Privacy advocates, however, are angered; claiming that mere surveys of privacy practices of online companies are insufficient. House Commerce Committee Chairman Representative Tom Bliley states, "Electronic commerce changes so quickly, I am con-

2. http://www.nytimes.com/library/tech/99/10/biztech/articles/11priv.html.
3. http://www.nytimes.com/library/tech/99/07/cyber/articles/13privacy.html.

cerned that a government mandated privacy policy would stifle innovation."

• **July 28, 1999.** The Clinton Administration announces a plan for the development of a Federal Intrusion Detection Network, or Fidnet, that would be used by the Federal Bureau of Investigation (FBI) to protect the nation's critical data networks from terrorists and intruders. Civil liberties groups, however, voice concern that the system could be the foundation for a surveillance network that could be misused and would itself be liable to attack.

• **July 1999.** In its 1999 report to Congress on self-regulation, the FTC concludes that voluntary practices were working adequately and that "no legislative action is necessary at this time."[4] However, citing a gap as large as 89 percent between the number of Internet sites that gather personal information and those that post a meaningful privacy policy, FTC Commissioner Sheila F. Anthony wrote that self-regulation "is not enough if the privacy practices themselves are toothless."

• **December 2, 1999.** According to a report issued by Forrester Research, Inc., some experts believed that the FTC would be forced by consumer advocates in the next twelve to eighteen months to pass a privacy bill of rights. However, Forrester has its doubts this would happen because of "profile-driven e-commerce" fueled by online marketing firms. (As of this writing, the FTC has not passed a privacy bill of rights for consumers; meanwhile, the conflict between marketers who create online profiles of consumers and privacy advocates who decry such practices carries

---

4. http://www.nytimes.com/library/tech/99/08/biztech/articles/30digi.html.

on.) Forrester's study of 10,000 North American households showed that 67 percent of Internet users are very concerned about giving data online, and 50 percent are ready for the government to intervene.

• **December 28, 1999.** The FTC announces the formation of the Advisory Committee on Online Access and Security, a group of thirty people representing consumer and business interests, to examine industry privacy efforts and define security standards that would enable consumers to access information collected about them.

• **January 13, 2000.** The Clinton Administration relaxes the restriction on the export of products containing stronger data encryption than previously allowed.

• **May 19, 2000.** The FTC decides to ask Congress for authority to impose tougher consumer privacy safeguards. This action was based on the results of a commission survey that showed only 20 percent of the major companies on the Internet had sufficient standards for protecting the privacy of Internet users.

• **May 23, 2000.** Reacting lukewarmly to the FTC's latest request for increased authority, the White House opposes the request of Robert Pitofsky, FTC chairman, to allow greater governmental control over privacy.

• **May 2000.** The FTC issues its third report that, while acknowledging progress made by the online industry to self-regulate, requests that Congress enact legislation in addition to the continued effort to self-regulate to ensure the protection of consumer online privacy. The FTC has not reported to Congress since the May 2000 report.

Fair Information Practices in the Electronic Marketplace

Although the FTC has shown interest in the issue of consumer privacy, it has also shown reluctance if not ambivalence about involving itself too deeply in the issue of consumer online privacy. Critics of "government interference"—most notably corporations with a vested interest in the continued expansion of the electronic economy such as Microsoft and IBM—have argued persuasively that overregulation of the online economy will stifle growth and dampen the enthusiasm of businesses and consumers alike to embrace this new business model.

However, the FTC also recognizes that unless something is done to address the consumer's growing concern over the privacy issue, the online economy could return once more to its former status of an "offline" economy in which consumer trust of the electronic transfer of personal data is deemed too risky and consumers return to the "brick-and-mortar" storefronts that protect privacy by permitting anonymous shopping and payments with cash. Citing the Georgetown Internet Privacy Policy Survey of the busiest 100 sites on the Internet, the FTC in its May 2000 report, "Fair Information Practices in the Electronic Marketplace," states that only 10 percent of those sites touched on the four fair information practices.[5] Again, these practices are:

1. **Notice/Awareness.** In general, the Web site should tell the user how it collects and handles user information. The notice should be conspicuous, and the privacy policy should clearly state

---

5. http://www.ftc.gov/os/2000/05/index.htm#22.

what information the site collects, how it collects it (e.g., forms, cookies, etc.), and how it uses it (e.g., is information sold to market research firms, available to meta-search engines, etc.?). Also, the policy should state how the site provides the other "fair practices": choice, access, and security.

2.   **Choice/Consent.** Web sites must give consumers control over how their personally identifying information is used. This includes marketing directly to the consumer, activities such as "purchase circles" (surreptitiously collecting buyer information based on ZIP code and e-mail addresses to make recommendations for products to other customers sharing the same attributes—ZIP code, city, company affiliation, etc.)—which Amazon.com implemented in 1999 and subsequently allowed customers to opt out of because of public concern[6]—and selling information to external companies such as market research firms. The primary problem found here is collecting information for one purpose and using it for another.

3.   **Access/Participation.** Perhaps the most controversial of the fair practices: users would be able to review, correct, and in some cases delete personally identifying information on a particular Web site. Inaccurate information or information used out of context can ruin a user's life.

4.   **Security/Integrity.** A topic unto itself (for an in-depth study of this issue, please see our *Complete Guide to Internet Security*): Web sites must do more than reassure users that their

6. "Amazon.com Revamps Privacy Policy." *Computerworld.* August 27, 1999. http://www.computerworld.com/cwi/story/0,1199,NAV47_STO28780,00. html.

information is secure with a "feel-good" policy statement. The site must implement policies, procedures, and tools that will prevent anything from unauthorized access to personal information to hostile attacks against the site. Of greatest concern is the loss of financial information such as credit card numbers, bank account numbers, etc.

There are several points worth noting about the fair practices. First, they antedate the Internet, having been developed by government agencies in Canada, Europe, and the United States since 1973. The concepts are neither new nor revelatory: they are the same practices being applied to the online medium. Second, the practices are couched in general terms. They are intentionally "technology neutral" to ensure their applicability to any platform while remaining meaningful.

However, a recent FTC survey showed that only 10 percent of all Web sites (as well as less than half of the 100 most popular Web sites) follow these fair information practices. This alarming trend has spurred many consumer advocacy groups to seek greater government involvement in the protection of consumer privacy.

Moving Toward Online Privacy Regulation

Based on the FTC's June 2000 report, the likelihood of increased government regulation to protect consumer online privacy is great. In July 2000, the FTC filed a lawsuit against Toysmart.com, the failed dotcom that once sold children's toys, asking that the company be prevented from selling customer information. The FTC claimed that Toysmart.com was violating its own privacy policy of protecting the privacy rights of their customers by selling children's names, birth dates, toy preferences, etc. Although Toysmart claimed that such information is a corporate asset that they need to sell to help liquidate their debt, the FTC saw things differently.

The FTC is taking a similar stance toward two more failed Internet companies, Boo.com and CraftShop.com, who were caught trying to sell credit card numbers, addresses, and other customer profiling information. Other major Internet presences such as Amazon.com and its subsidiary, Alexa, are also facing lawsuits and inquiries launched by the FTC. Could this be a case of the irresponsible few casting doubt on the ability of the industry as a whole to self-regulate, or is it an industry unchecked that is running amok?

Earlier complaints against DoubleClick Inc. for its use of Web bugs (to track the actions of Web surfers) and a class action suit against America Online (for tracking downloads of .exe and .zip files) are making it increasingly difficult for the government to turn a blind eye to the growing volume of consumer complaints about their invasion of privacy. The result has been an increasing number of Internet privacy bills currently before Congress—as of this writing over 300 bills, the purpose of which is to regulate everything from the use of medical records to the protection of children's rights.

Two of the more prominent bills are the Consumer Privacy Protection Act sponsored by Senator Ernest Hollings, D-S.C., and a bill by Senator John Kerry, D.-Mass. The Consumer Privacy Protection Act requires, among other things, that consumers must give companies permission before their personal information can be collected, and they must also have the choice to opt out of giving personal information. The Kerry bill requires "clear and conspicuous disclosure of Web sites' privacy policies." It entrusts enforcement of privacy guidelines to state attorneys general, who are required to notify the FTC of any violations prior to prosecuting. Kerry's bill also calls for the formation of an independent commission to monitor progress of self-regulation and to report to Congress any progress made at the end of the year. It is seen as a compromise between the current *laissez-faire* attitude of the Federal government and a growing call for strict government regulation.

Even though a group of fifty companies surveyed by Forrester Research, Inc. states that they use customer information primarily for internal analysis (see Figure 1-2), the FTC has not been dissuaded from pursuing a more vigorous role in legislating privacy protection.

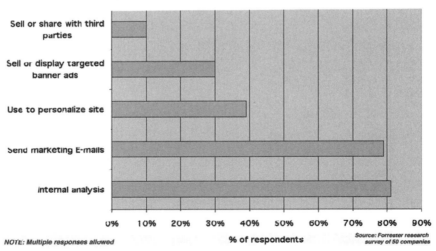

Figure 1-2   How Customer Data Is Used

What do you do with the customer information you collect online?

NOTE: Multiple responses allowed   % of respondents   Source: Forrester research survey of 50 companies

Privacy Laws Are Becoming Imminent

Pending legislation in Congress focuses on three major areas of the privacy issue, according to *InformationWeek* magazine:

• What information are companies collecting about their customers?

• Should controls be instituted only when customer information is sold to third parties, or should controls be instituted regardless of who uses it?

• Should online businesses be required to manage customer data differently from brick-and-mortar businesses as data management practices relate to privacy? One complaint that the online business community is making is that stricter data privacy standards are being applied to them than to the traditional business world (i.e., non-Internet or offline businesses).

Odds are that every company that transacts business on the Internet will be experiencing more rather than less regulation as time goes on despite the general opposition of corporate America to increased regulation (see Figure 1-3).

Figure 1-3 Opposition to Government's Role

Should the government set online privacy policies?

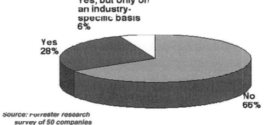

Yes, but only on an industry-specific basis 6%

Yes 28%

No 66%

Source: Forrester research survey of 50 companies

Opting for Self-Regulation

Businesses concerned about increasing levels of government involvement in privacy matters are promoting self-regulation over federal legislation. Let's take a look at some of the reasoning behind self-regulation, and at the policies and tools that companies can use to help reassure their customers that their information is safe.

One of the organizations at the forefront of promoting self-regulation over further government regulation is the Online Privacy Alliance (OPA). Formed in April 1998, the OPA represents over 100 corporations including America Online, IBM, Hewlett-Packard, Microsoft, and other trade associations that originally met in reaction to an FTC report citing the shortcomings of self-regulation. Christine Varney, who ironically enough was the FTC's Internet activist until she left in August 1997 to join OPA, heads the organization.

The OPA promotes self-regulation over no regulation or excessive government regulation. In testimony before the Senate Committee on Commerce, Science, and Transportation in May 2000, Varney stated that OPA felt that FTC's surveys citing a lack of Web site compliance of Fair Privacy Practices are inaccurate. She also claimed that existing legislation to protect consumer privacy, including the Medical Financial Privacy Protection Act and the Children's Online Privacy Protection Act, is sufficient, and that further legislation would only hamper the growth of Internet commerce while providing no additional safeguards for the consumer.[7]

Varney voices the concerns of many champions of electronic commerce, including higher-ups in the federal government, who

7. http://www.privacyalliance.org/resources/varney_testimony05252000.shtml.

feel that the federal government cannot pass legislation quickly enough to match the speed at which technology innovates and reinvents itself. Rather, the OPA has adopted a series of self-regulatory policies, modeled closely after the Fair Information Practices, which a member organization must adopt at a minimum upon joining the OPA. These policies are outlined below[8]:

1.   **Adoption and Implementation of a Privacy Policy.** An organization actively engaged in online business or electronic commerce must adopt policies and practices aimed at protecting the privacy of consumers. The organization should also share their "best practices" with business partners and encourage them to implement the same policies and procedures.

2.   **Notice and Disclosure.** The privacy policy must be readily accessible to the individual, and must identify the information that is being collected, how it is being used, whether or not it will be distributed in part or in whole to a third party (e.g., a marketing research firm), the choices the individual has related to the collection of the information, the organization's data security policy, and the steps the organization will take to ensure the reliability of the data. Finally, the notice should let the user know how to contact the organization in the event of a complaint or question.

3.   **Choice/Consent.** More familiarly known as "opt in/opt out," the user must be able to control how a company uses personally identifying information for reasons other than its expressly advertised purpose. Also, the user must be able to opt out if the company intends to distribute this information to a third party for reasons other than the reasons cited.

8. http://www.privacyalliance.org/resources/ppguidelines.shtml.

4. **Data Security**. The company must operate a secure Web site that guarantees that unauthorized individuals, both internal and external, cannot access personally identifying information and misuse it in any way (e.g., alteration, deletion, loss). Securing a Web site is no small task, and is the subject of several other chapters in this book.

5. **Data Quality and Access**. Companies that collect and maintain personally identifying information must be able to vouch for the completeness, reliability, timeliness, and accuracy of the information they keep. The methods they use to collect the information must be sound, and the process followed to collect information should be simple and fast.

In addition, the OPA endorses other steps that a company must take in order to effectively enforce online privacy policies. Regardless of whether this enforcement is self-imposed or performed by a third party or seal program (see Chapter 9 for more on seal programs), the company must perform the following as important steps toward self-regulation:

1. Continually verify and monitor privacy policies.

2. Resolve customer complaints quickly.

3. Educate customers about their roles and responsibilities in privacy matters and how they can help protect themselves.

How a company chooses to follow these steps, whether through self-enforcement or through the services of a third party, is up to the individual organization. This decision depends upon the cost of developing and maintaining privacy policies internally (as opposed to using a third party), the availability of in-house expertise, and the willingness or ability of a business to contract with outside companies. Regardless of how these policies are enforced, what really matters is that the policies live up to the expectations of the public and the FTC. Otherwise, companies that choose not to adopt some sort of self-regulatory policies will turn the job over to someone else who may not understand internal organizational policies and procedures as well as in-house resources. In Chapter 7 you'll see what you can do to begin implementing your own privacy policies.

A Diagnostic for Privacy Controls

Before you can create and implement a sound privacy policy, you must first understand what these policies mean; second, you must assess how your company stands in relation to these policies. Before rushing off to pay for expensive consulting services and software, you need to understand what it is you are trying to protect.

The United States Council for International Business (USCIB) recently published a "privacy diagnostic" that will assist companies in this effort. The USCIB states that "in order to avoid governmental solutions that will be less workable than effective self-regulation, all sectors of U.S. business must address this [privacy] issue." Included in the diagnostic is a series of questions intended to make companies think about the data they collect and how they use it. A summary of the diagnostic (which can be found in greater detail at the USCIB's Web site, www.uscib.org) follows:

• What information that you collect from customers may be considered personally identifiable information, and what do you do with it once you have it?

• How is both internal data (e.g., data about your employees) and external data (e.g., data about your customers) collected?

• Who should be involved in the gathering of personally identifiable information and the corporate decision making process?

• Who controls the information once it is collected?

• How and where is the information stored? Is it stored centrally, or is it distributed? Does the storage location differ from the collection location?

• Why is the information being collected in the first place? Was the primary purpose for the collection disclosed to the customer?

• How is the information being used? Is it used only for the reason disclosed, or is it being used for other purposes?

• Will the information be transferred within the company, or sold to or shared with a third party? Was this policy disclosed to the customer?

• Does your company currently have existing standards, guidelines, or regulations that cover the collection, control, or transfer of the information?

• Does your company have a grievance process in place? Is it publicized and clearly communicated, both internally and externally?

• Do you understand the basic privacy principles of limiting the scope of information collection, data quality, purpose and intent, use limitation, security, accessibility of policy, ability to correct information, and overall accountability for information collection policies?

• Finally, do you understand the principles of international privacy protection and the importance of maintaining an uninterrupted, free flow of data across borders?

The answers to these questions will help you to begin understanding the degree of "toxicity" of the collected data and lead you to discovering what controls are necessary to prevent an environmental disaster from occurring in the event of an accidental "leak." Throughout the book you'll find different types of compensating controls to prevent or contain any damage you may experience.

Why Privacy Policies Should Matter

We have entered an age of seemingly unlimited computing power and sophisticated data gathering techniques unheard of just a few years ago. Online companies are now capable of creating startlingly detailed and accurate composite profiles of individuals from a number of different sources, often unbeknownst to the individual. This development has not escaped the attention of the American public. According to the FTC, 92 percent of Americans show concern about their privacy and how personal information is used,[9] and that concern is not likely to abate. And unless online companies can convince the public that their personal information is safe, they will abandon the Internet for more secure and anonymous—and offline—ways of conducting business.

Obviously, this is something that nobody wants to see happen, not the online companies, not the federal government, not

9. Gary Clayton,Figure 66-2   DLE. Note the extensive alopecia and scarring evident in this case.

the individual who increasingly turns to the Internet for everything from online purchasing to personal finances. Companies must do more than simply post privacy policies on their sites. They must be able to answer questions such as those posed by the USCIB, identify the individuals within the organization responsible for data collection and use, formulate policies and procedures, and act on them.

What about international concerns? Clearly the FTC can't regulate beyond U.S. borders, but privacy is a universal concern. And just how legitimate is this concern? We now need to look at some of the ways in which technology is being used to complicate the privacy issue.

Privacy Under Attack

If the online consumer has any doubts that his privacy is under attack, all he needs to do is to look at his junk mail inbox. He didn't solicit information on refinancing his mortgage, consolidating his debt, or buying a timeshare in Florida, and yet his electronic inbox is full of such unsolicited advertisements. If he's thinking his life is secure and private, he needs to rethink his position.

Consider this e-mail advertisement for PCSpy2000:

PCSpy2000

Learn EVERYTHING about your friends, neighbors, enemies, employees, co-workers, even your boss, even yourself!

Unlock incredible hidden secrets and more! Investigate anyone and everyone from the privacy of your own home. This program allows you to tap into the very same information

---

sources that are used by Professional Private Investigators! Track, Locate, or conduct a Complete Background Check on ANYONE, at ANY TIME! Quick, Easy, and Private. All the info you want is just a few mouse clicks away!

Find License Plate Numbers!

- Get anyone's name and address with just a license plate number! (Find that guy or girl you met in traffic!)

- Business records! Get complete business records!

- Social security numbers! Trace anyone by his or her social security number!

- Unlisted phone numbers! Get anyone's phone number with just a name—even unlisted numbers!

- Locate! Long lost friends, relatives, a past lover who broke your heart!

- E-mail! Send anonymous e-mail completely untraceable!

- Dirty secrets! Discover dirty secrets your in-laws don't want you to know!

- Ex-spouse! Learn how to get information on an ex-spouse that will help you win in court!

- Criminal search background check! Find out about your daughter's boyfriend!

- Find out about yourself! Are you being investigated?

- Neighbors! Learn all about your mysterious neighbors! Find out what they have to hide!

- Coworkers! Be astonished by what you'll learn about people you work with!

- Education verification! DID he really graduate college? Find out!

    The PC Spy 2000 Software will help you discover ANY-THING about anyone, with clickable hyperlinks and no typing in Internet addresses! Just run the software and Go! DIFFERENT INFORMATION SECTIONS, TOOLS AND TOPICS OFFERED WITHIN THE PC Spy 2000

Tap Into Investigative Sources

How and where to investigate, perform, or locate:

- Credit information.
- Driver's records.
- Lawsuit information, civil and criminal.
- Employment screening.
- Criminal records.
- Asset identification.
- Bounty hunter resources.
- Investigative information.
- Secrets of someone's past.
- Find tax liens, property records, vehicle ownership, and many other public records.
- Business records.
- Where to listen in on the police radios (scanner.)
- Check on doctors, lawyers or other professionals. Determine their track records.

Also within the PC Spy 2000 is a complete how-to section devoted to the topic of background investigations. What public sources are available and how you can use them.

Locate People—Find Almost Anyone

Lots of information, extensive contact sources, and even many tools that will allow you to:

- Find people who have relocated.
- Find people who have changed their name or address.
- Locate resources for adoption-related searches.
- Determine which locate source to use and how.
- Have the government locate deadbeat parents.
- Locate people using public records available to anyone.
- Locate military buddies.
- Find addresses using just a phone number.
- Create a map showing directions to a person's house.
- How to follow the paper trail almost everyone leaves.
- Use the same tips and tricks that investigators use when all else fails.
- Use the post office to determine the address behind a P.O. box.

The PC Spy 2000 not only provides the sources most useful in locating people but also offers a complete **"How To"** section that explains how and when to use the different sources and methods provided.

All this and more, for only $29.95!

The old saying that what you don't know won't hurt you is clearly an anachronism now. Unfortunately, many business people and software developers still believe they can violate customer privacy with impunity. It is hard to believe but the creators of the Web browsers we use today actually decided that collecting personal information about customers, without bothering to notify them, could be considered a consumer benefit. So rather than continually ask users for their user IDs and passwords each time they visited a particular site, Web browsers—beginning with Netscape in 1994—began collecting and saving personal information, all without alerting the user or bothering to ask for permission to do so.

The intentions of these software companies most likely were good. But developers were oblivious to the controversy that they would create just a few years later. The practice of tracking a customer's browsing and shopping habits on the Internet without notification has grown along with the sophistication of the Internet and electronic commerce, so much so that consumers and policymakers are becoming increasingly alarmed. According to an August 2000 survey by the Pew Internet and American Life, 54 percent of Internet users claim that online tracking of personal information and behaviors invades their privacy. This number does vary depending upon the age group surveyed, but the majority of those interviewed felt that online tracking was an invasion of their privacy (see Figure 1-4).

Furthermore, in the Pew Survey, 84 percent of those surveyed said they favor an "opt in" privacy policy that allows the user to specify the personal information a site may collect before the fact rather than after the fact. Opt in systems such as the Platform for Privacy Preferences, or P3P (discussed in Chapter 6), resemble European Union systems in which their omnibus privacy policies

Figure 1-4   Concern Over Online Tracking

Online Tracking

Young people are more likely to say online tracking is helpful, because the company can provide information that matches their interests.

	Helpful	Harmful
All Internet users	27%	54%
Ages 18-29	36%	47%
Ages 30-49	25%	54%
Ages 50-64	23%	56%

Source: Pew Internet & American Life Project. May-June 2000 Fall.

are designed to give the individual greater protection of his personal information than self-regulatory or opt out approaches that are commonly used in the United States. Two thirds of those surveyed felt that Web sites should not be allowed to track their online behavior at all, and a staggering 81 percent said that laws should be enacted to prevent this from happening.

The stakes are high and are getting higher according to the May 2000 FTC report to the U.S. Congress on the "Fair Information Practices in the Electronic Marketplace." Highlights of the report show the following:

• 92 percent of consumers remain concerned (67 percent are very concerned) about the misuse of their personal information through online channels.

• 76 percent of consumers who are not concerned about privacy in the offline world fear privacy intrusions on the Internet.

• Estimates of lost business due to consumer privacy concerns range from $2.8 billion today, upwards to $18 billion by 2002 if nothing is done to allay these fears.

• 92 percent of those surveyed state they don't trust online companies to keep their personal data confidential.

• 82 percent agreed that the government should regulate how companies use their personal information.

And yet, a growing number of consumers (64 percent of respondents to the Pew Survey) are willing to give personal information on the Internet: everything from e-mail addresses to birth dates, telephone numbers to credit card numbers. We appear to have a situation in which consumers' actions belie their words. They are afraid for their personal information and yet, more often than not, the pull and convenience of using the Internet is apparently too much to resist.

Cookies

Many consumers have heard of the term "cookie" in reference to the Internet, but few understand what they are or how they are used on their computer. We will discuss cookies at some length in Chapter 8. For now, let us say that cookies are text files that a Web site can place on a user's computer to harvest data about the user. The site might, for example, track user preferences and recommend similar products or services (as Amazon.com so expertly does). Sites may also collect more personally identifying information such as name, address, and social security and bank account numbers, and store it in a cookie file unbeknownst to the user. The fact that cookies are both hidden and persistent (i.e., they remain on a user's hard drive unless he deliberately deletes the file) has helped fuel the concern over how cookies are used.

Reversing the Trends

To build successful businesses, entrepreneurs must reassure customers that they can meaningfully protect their online privacy. By ensuring customer privacy, businesses can seal loyalty with the most precious gifts of all—freedom and trust.

Technology can help provide protection, but truly meaningful security results from sound business practices. Because privacy and security are two sides of the same e-commerce coin, you need to offer your customers the best of both.

Think of privacy as a pyramid (shown in Figure 1-5) that has three layers—policies, standards, and procedures that are needed to assure your customers that their concerns are being addressed.

DoubleClick on the Hot Seat

In January 2000, DoubleClick Inc. was sued, accused of unlawfully obtaining and selling consumers' personal information in their online advertising activities. They were charged with using cookies to track and record the sites an individual visits, as well as the information transmitted on the sites, such as names, ages, addresses, shopping patterns, and financial information.

Figure 1-5 The Privacy Pyramid

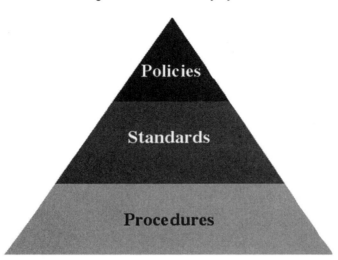

According to the suit, DoubleClick misrepresented itself by claiming they do not collect user information. The suit asked DoubleClick to stop collecting any further information and to provide the means for Internet users to destroy all personal information that it had already gathered about them.

Even Bankruptcy May Not Protect You

In July 2000, the U.S. Federal Trade Commission (FTC) sued the failed Web site Toysmart.com for deceptively offering for sale personal information about site visitors. Toysmart collected details about their customers, including names, addresses, billing information, preferences, and birth dates. Their privacy policy promised that "personal information. . . will never be shared with third parties." In May 2000,

Toysmart.com closed their doors and began to liquidate their assets—including lists of customers—in violation of their own policy.

Customer Expectations

If the golden rule applies anywhere, it's in today's e-commerce world—don't expect people to do anything that you would object to doing yourself. This principle takes on a multiple of dimensions, but can be boiled down into the following four:

- **Notice.** Tell people what personal data you intend to collect, how you intend to collect it (forms, cookies, etc.), how you'll use it, whether or not you'll share it with other companies, and whether or not other companies are collecting data on your site as customers move through it.

- **Choice.** Offer people a choice as to how you use their personal information beyond consummating a sale (marketing to them or selling their information to third parties).

- **Access.** Provide your customers reasonable access to see what information you've collected about them, and offer them opportunities to fix it or delete it when the data is inaccurate or they deem that you no longer have a right to use it.

- **Security.** Protect customer data as though your life depends on it (in reality, your livelihood does!).

Although these steps may seem like a tall order, don't be dismayed or discouraged. Throughout the book you'll see that the benefits of responsible information handling practices far outweigh the pain of ensuring their presence.

Minding your customers' privacy is more than just a good idea—it's imperative! Those who fail to heed the industry's call for privacy protections now are likely to face a grim future, especially when you're called before a judge who's not very sympathetic.

Rather than jumping to the conclusion that online shoppers are sniveling complainers who expect everything and offer little in return, put yourself into your customer's shoes first and take a close look at your operations from their point of view. You'll quickly see that their expectations are the very same as your own.

The other companies within your chain of supply that keep your e-commerce gears turning share your customers' concerns for privacy, but include several other concerns that may not be obvious. Chapter 2 takes a look at business-to-business (B2B) e-commerce concerns that may affect you if you engage in electronic marketplace sales and purchasing.

Business-to-Business and Electronic Marketplace Privacy and Security Concerns

Neglecting privacy in business-to-business (B2B) electronic marketplaces is a certain one-way ticket to landing in hot water with a government or civil action. If there's willful negligence involved—such as collecting information for one purpose and knowingly using for another, colluding with other marketplace members to limit membership into the market, price fixing, price change signaling, or any other kind of monkey business— you could easily wind up in a criminal court, too! In academic terms, an electronic marketplace (e-market) is where buyers and suppliers with a common interest (e.g., a vertical industry such as aircraft parts) agree to enter an electronic shopping and buying club of sorts in which suppliers bid for your business, and you're offered a wider variety of potential sources, along with stream-lined efficiencies and reduced costs for all purchases.

E-markets are characterized as a B2B integrated supplier exchange that is accessible through a single global portal, where the goal is to eliminate redundancies and processing burdens from suppliers by integration and collaboration, thus leading to lower cost, easier business practices, and a marked increase in efficiencies for an entire industry.

Because heterogeneous data is necessarily entrusted to partners within a B2B e-market, the stakes become considerably higher, and even simple mistakes could lead to a leakage of data that no trading partner participant would ever tolerate.

Should accidental disclosure of confidential pricing agreements or sensitive custom catalog data leak out from a member's Web site to other buyers or other suppliers who should not see such data, and that problem is due to a mistake or misconfiguration problem on your Web site, your suppliers' other customers may cry foul or wind up ending their business relationships with your supplier altogether. If careless handling on your part caused this breach, you may bear some of the liability and be asked to make up the differences in lost sales. In March 2000, Sony Corp. announced that the personal data of customers who had ordered the PlayStation2 online had been leaked from a Sony Web site to other customers who used their own passwords to gain access to the site. Forty-four customers who logged onto the PlayStation.com site with their own passwords and identification numbers gained information for other customers such as their names, addresses, and the amounts of ordered consoles, a Sony Computer Entertainment Inc. (SCE) spokeswoman said. According to a 3 March 2000, report from IDG News Service, information for 266 customers was revealed. "In cases where we find actual damage to our customers' privacy, we would take proper actions including payment of compensation," a Sony spokesperson said.

Is it really worth the risk?

In the B2B arena, security and privacy controls become essential and are increasingly becoming mandated long before access to participation in an e-market is granted.

B2B E-Markets

Some of the common problems found with privacy and security in B2B markets include:

• Failure to protect sensitive data, including custom catalog pricing; sales, transaction, and payment data; bids; and auction data.

• Failure to build sufficient levels of trust in the security or performance of e-commerce from external partners, leading to an inability to maintain any sales or volume quotas needed to maintain membership in the network. Should your site be deemed untrustworthy because of previous compromises, or poor results from a vulnerability analysis exercise that a B2B market manager may have mandated to maintain membership in the e-market, customers will likely be disinclined to place sensitive data on your site, leading to a loss in sales. Other problems here include a lack of strong user authentication mechanisms, maintaining others' data securely, or failure to meet your promises of shipping dates, quantities, etc.

• Lock-out of markets abroad due to a lack of adopting the more restrictive and comprehensive privacy principles that are being mandated by most foreign governments (see Chapter 4).

For the moment, let's look at a basic model of B2B e-commerce to point out where privacy and security issues exist.

Corporate Internet Purchasing

In Chapter 1, the emphasis was on consumer-related e-shopping experiences in which privacy problems occur because of the strong needs for highly personalized Web user experiences. Now consider what privacy concerns may lie within the B2B purchasing environment. Here we'll examine what types of activities occur within a corporate purchasing environment for maintenance, repair, and operations (MRO) goods and services, then examine how e-markets can help to eliminate many of the associated problems with corporate purchasing systems.

The employees at the Acme Corporation complain steadily because the supply room is always empty of critical supplies: ballpoint pens, paper clips, and business envelopes. The purchasing department is obligated to control procurement of these essential supplies, so they have managed to strike a deal with their suppliers, committing to an entire year's supply of goods at a hefty volume discount. This business model, while appearing straightforward to an outsider, introduces several problems that involve internal procedures, controls, and technology, and that affect privacy.

• Who does the ordering? Obviously, the purchasing department doesn't want a thousand employees placing thousands of different purchase orders—it would be too difficult to ensure there were no fraudulent orders or orders placed with nonapproved vendors.

• Which online supplier should store the catalog and buyer information? If your suppliers maintain information about your employees on their systems, how can you know that they're adequately protecting it for you and preventing it from being used for purposes other than what you intended?

So with all these potential problems, why are businesses rushing out to purchase on the Internet? Simple: Internet purchasing is more efficient and it saves money! How much more efficiently? "Shift purchasing to the Web, and a business can eliminate 90 percent of transaction costs," claims Dean Whitlock, vice president and general manager of consulting firm ICL's eBusiness Services group in Dallas. A more modest though still impressive estimate comes from Chris Cogan, CEO of GoCo-op, a Florida-based Internet purchasing solution for hotels, restaurants, and healthcare businesses. "The average cost of executing a paper purchase order is $115," he says. "We get that cost down to $10. When companies buy through our system, they'll see immediate savings."

Serpents in the Garden of Efficiencies

In an 18 September 2000, online edition of *Computerworld Magazine*, Carol Sliwa asked FTC member Mozelle W. Thompson if he noticed any differences between B2B and business-to-consumer (B2C) issues that come before him; here's what he had to say: "What's really interesting about B2B and B2C is that there's greater convergence to how people are beginning to regard these issues. A lot of people believe that, for example, the idea of consumer privacy is a pure B2C issue and companies that are really in the B2B space don't have to worry about it. Well it's not that simple. It's an information practices issue. It's how you gather and use information. And I think that businesses that are in the B2B space are beginning to recognize that their customers are asking them: How are you using my information? Where's it going and what are you doing with it?" As reports of misused information strike fear into the hearts of buyers and sellers alike, privacy concerns dominate business relationships regardless of the medium used for exchange. Although B2B proves its value with each transaction conducted, the chain of trust is only as good as the weakest link, and everyone becomes responsible for prudent uses of the technology and the information it manages.

In spite of the reduced costs and added efficiencies, the potential for antitrust and anticompetitive problems in B2B markets has piqued the interest of the FTC. While the FTC isn't in any great hurry to impose tight regulations, they've made it crystal clear that if exchanges begin to behave as cartels, monopolies, monopsonies, or breach the privacy of participant companies or fail to maintain the appropriate levels of information security, these companies might wind up in an antitrust action against them.

What's a Monopsony?

According to the Economic Gloss*arama, a monopsony is a market characterized by a single buyer of a product. A good example of a monopsony is the Central Selling Organization (CSO), the diamond-buying arm of De Beers. Since the 1930s, it has bought up about 80 percent of the value of world diamond production and then (acting as a monopoly) regulates the amount of diamonds it sells on the market. Monopsony is the buying-side equivalent of a selling-side monopoly. Where a monopoly describes a single seller in a specific market, a monopsony is a single buyer. Like a monopoly seller, a monopsony buyer is a price maker with complete market control. Monopsony is also comparable to a monopoly in terms of inefficiency. Monopsony does not generate an efficient allocation of resources. The price paid by a monopsony is lower and the quantity exchanged is less than would be had if the market were perfectly competitive.

The U.S. government is increasing its interest in electronic marketplaces, especially the FTC. In June 2000, they sponsored the first FTC workshop on competition policy in the world of B2B electronic marketplaces to determine if problems in consumer-to-consumer sites bleeds over to B2B marketplaces, and to determine what unique problems are found in B2B markets.

"The promise of huge efficiencies from B2B is certainly tantalizing. On the other hand, I can't help but wonder if there might be a serpent in the garden of efficiencies," said FTC Commissioner Sheila Anthony in her remarks before the workshop, expressing her concerns that buying and selling efficiency could easily introduce unfair or lax business practices, leading to FTC actions or privacy and security problems.

Beginning in 2000, the U.S. government began looking closely at B2B e-markets and seeking input from the industry to help them both understand the landscape and prepare to regulate it more closely should it become necessary. In April 2000, the FTC and the U.S. Department of Justice jointly published the *Antitrust Guidelines for Collaborations Among Competitors* as guidance on how to avoid certain problems (see sidebar).

FTC and DOJ Issue Antitrust Guidelines for Collaborations Among Competitors

The FTC and the Antitrust Division of the U.S. Department of Justice (DOJ) have issued the *Antitrust Guidelines for Collaborations Among Competitors*. They are the first set of guidelines issued jointly by both federal antitrust agencies that address a broad range of horizontal agreements among competitors, including joint ventures, strategic alliances, and other competitor collaborations. The guidelines describe an analytical framework to assist businesses in assessing the likelihood of an antitrust challenge to a collaboration with one or more competitors.

Competitive forces of globalization and technology are driving firms toward complex collaborations to achieve goals such as expanding into foreign markets, funding expensive innovation efforts, and lowering production and other costs. The increasing varieties and use of collaborations by rivals have yielded requests for improved clarity regarding their treatment under the antitrust laws.

"The 'Competitor Collaboration Guidelines' provide sound analytical guidance for a business environment characterized by increasing collaborative activity," FTC Chairman Robert Pitofsky said. "The guidelines will help businesses assess the antitrust implications of collaborations with rivals, thereby encouraging pro-competitive collaborations and deterring collaborations likely to harm competition and consumers." Their intent is to encourage B2B marketplaces while helping to ensure that participants don't use the technology to prevent fair competition among partners.

Although these guidelines aren't strictly for B2B e-commerce, the rapid growth in B2B online marketplaces has accelerated the development of these guidelines.

Finding the Roots of Privacy Problems

Privacy problems in the B2B marketplace often appear because of lax computer security practices that lead to leakage or poor storage. To best determine whether your site is afflicted, you'll need to conduct a self-discovery exercise.

Are You Compliant?

Information sharing between buyers and suppliers (order data, custom pricing and volume agreement, etc.) and within B2B e-markets has the potential for causing concerns and should force you to ask yourself these questions:

• Could specific information I collect and accidentally (or willfully) divulge point to collusive activity?

• Is information I provide already available through other sources, or does the ease or speed of releasing the information through the marketplace make it more valuable to some participants than to others? As an example, could knowing a change in price or availability of a product earlier than other members of the marketplace be considered anticompetitive?

• Are policies, processes, firewalls, and other security and privacy mechanisms in place to limit the exchange of competitively significant information (custom pricing, order details, delivery commitments, etc.) without interfering with the functioning of the site or the marketplace?

FTC Warning Signs

The FTC has already begun to scrutinize supply-chain trading networks for anticompetitive activities like price signaling (sharing changes in pricing with a select few participants), collusion (two or more buyers ganging up on a supplier to force specific activity), and freezing out competitors. Legal experts at the FTC recommend that traders maintain secure enough systems to keep pricing and trade secrets confidential. They further recommend that firewalls be used to keep catalog, pricing, and bids safe from prying eyes of competitors within the exchange.

Some red flags that the FTC says will get you into hot water with both anticompetitive practices and privacy issues when participating in a B2B exchange:

• Allowing competitors to see one another's prices in electronic catalogs and auctions.

• Allowing competitors to signal future price increases or discounts to selected customers, thus revealing confidential information that would otherwise benefit everyone in a "fair" marketplace.

• Unfairly restricting who can join an exchange or prohibiting participants from joining other exchanges by using externally supplied data for purposes other than what the supplier intended and agreed to.

• Allowing competitors to openly discuss private pricing agreements, outputs, costs, or strategic plans on forums or discussion boards that you offer as a service on your B2B site. If restricted access to these discussion boards is limited to a select group of customers and suppliers, you may be accused of openly sharing sensitive data, or of forming a cartel.

E-Market Operating Standards

Following the workshop, the FTC solicited public comments from any interested parties and posted them on its Web site (www.ftc.gov). In their public comments following the FTC's B2B Workshop, Ernst and Young, LLP (E&Y), a leader in helping businesses establish and maintain the infrastructures and practices needed for responsible membership in B2B markets, emphasized the need for a comprehensive and robust self-regulatory framework for industry-wide security and privacy practices, and recommended the FTC help to both develop and establish a gold standard for e-business and use the standard to measure compliance. With these standards, e-business participants will be required to follow four principles for managing customers' e-privacy expectations: notice, choice, access, and security, for B2B customers as well as your B2C customers. In addition, e-business operating standards need to address the following concerns to effectively allay the fears of stakeholders in electronic marketplaces:

- Neutrality

- Confidentiality

- Security

- Availability

- Transparency

Neutrality

By maintaining their openness to new participants who can enter or leave the exchange as they choose without strict controls, e-markets limit their risks of forming exclusionary cartels that may ultimately fall under the FTC's investigative microscope.

Confidentiality

Maintaining the confidence of members within the exchange with security and privacy controls, e-markets can limit their risks of disclosing sensitive information (trade secrets, custom pricing agreements, etc.) to other competitors or customers because of lax security or improper handling. These leaks of information could cause an undesirable shift in the balance of the marketplace where "insider" information impedes fair competition, and begins to eliminate competitors or customers who become victims of the leaked data. Maintaining confidentiality requires strong user authentication among participants to enable the controlled flow of mission-critical data with the confidence of its users.

Security

Security needs to be all-encompassing and provide for prevention, detection, and reaction mechanisms for enforcing security. Specifically you need to be thinking about confidentiality and preventing the users within a marketplace or rogue hackers from accessing or exploring the marketplace or from using a participant's Web site to launch an attack on another participant because of Web server vulnerabilities left wide open. Because hacking attacks are difficult to trace, an attack on a competitor's site from a vulnerable Web server that you maintain could be interpreted as an "act of war" and could escalate into a nasty legal battle.

Availability

Maintaining the presence and availability of an e-market's Web site becomes a greater concern to partners who begin to rely on the market to fulfill the needs of manufacturing and for MRO goods and services. As mission-critical relationships develop over time, it becomes essential that products and services are available when they're needed. When partners include companies from abroad, there's little room for downtime and the sun never really sets.

Transparency

Members must use uniform standards for data formats and data content to ensure transparency of B2B exchanges. Otherwise transactions require layer upon layer of data conversions each time a new supplier or buyer is added to the exchange. The eXtensible Markup Language (XML) is one example of a data management standard that adds to efficiencies (through common data exchange types and formats) and can also help with elements of security, confidentiality, sender authentication, and message integrity. For more on how XML can enhance the security of a B2B exchange, see the sidebar on IBM's XML Security Suite

Product Profile: IBM XML Security Suite

XML is being used to solve even the stickiest of Internet communications problems. IBM's contribution is the XML Security Suite.

At the heart of the suite you'll find DOMHASH as a reference implementation for computing digital signatures on XML documents. IBM is offering the XML Security Suite as the basis for the digital signature discussions occurring at both the Internet Engineering Task Force (IETF) and the World Wide Web Consortium (W3C). IBM provides support for element-wise encryption on XML data, digital signatures on entire XML documents, and access control features that aren't possible under SSL transport layer security.

DOMHASH is intended as a canonicalizer (reduces to canonical terms) for XML digital signatures. The sample implementation provided with the security suite is based on a draft submitted to the IETF. You can download the XML Security Suite (for free) from IBM's alphaWorks site at www.alphaWorks.ibm.com in the Resources: Tools section. For B2B e-commerce to supplant traditional, costly, and time consuming exchanges with low-cost and readily available Internet technology, the security of business documents must be ramped up considerably and comprehensively. With digitally signed documents, both senders and receivers are assured that messages originated at their advertised source and no tampering of message contents occurred en route.

Clearly, B2B participation is not for the faint of heart, and those wanting to step into the ballpark need to prepare themselves for widespread changes in policies, processes, practices, and technologies.

In Chapter 3, we turn to privacy problems in the workplace.

Workplace Matters

In his 1787 doctrine "Panopticon," Utilitarian philosopher Jeremy Bentham outlined his design for a system meant to bring order to chaotic systems of law and social welfare. "Panopticon," or "The Inspection House," was literally a house designed to keep workers, prisoners, and others under surveillance. The circular building Bentham designed (see Figure 3-1) housed a centrally located inspector who could watch the "inmates" without being seen.[1]

The modern-day threat of an electronic Panopticon has alarmed privacy advocates who feel that, much like the workers in Bentham's model, the modern-day office worker's every move can be watched and tracked without his ever knowing it. The only difference in their eyes is that the physical model has been replaced with a more insidious electronic version that allows employers to read their employees' e-mail, record keystrokes, listen

---

1. http://www.dnai.com/~mackey/thesis/panpic.html.

Figure 3-1   Bentham's "Panopticon"

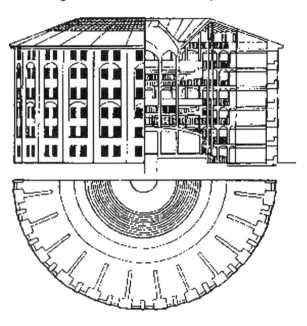

in on phone conversations, access their files, and track the Web sites they visit while on company time.

Workers have every reason to worry. According to an April 2000 survey conducted by the American Management Association (AMA), almost three quarters (73.5 percent) of major U.S. firms said they monitored their employees' e-mail, computer files, and telephone calls, up from 35 percent two years earlier. Furthermore, one quarter of the firms surveyed said they had fired employees for improper use of electronic tools.[2]

The AMA concluded from its survey that the larger the company, the more likely it is to monitor its employees' behaviors. Financial services such as banks, brokerage firms, and insurance

2. http://www.amanet.org/research/specials/elecmont.htm.

companies lead all other industries in monitoring employees' e-mail (55 percent) and the Web sites they visit (73 percent).

Employers who monitor their employees offer a number of reasons to defend their behavior. Many employers feel that although advances in technology in the workplace are designed to increase worker productivity, they can also be a drag on performance. They argue that they need to monitor employee behaviors and determine how much time they are doing real work as opposed to surfing the Web for entertainment or conducting personal business. How much time are employees spending sending or receiving personal e-mail, visiting Amazon.com, or placing off-track bets, or talking on the telephone to friends or family members when they should be conducting company business?

Companies with a policy of monitoring their employees' behaviors further argue, perhaps more convincingly, that the myriad of electronic tools sitting on the employee's desk also exposes the company to litigation and other legal risks, not to mention the potential loss of company confidential and proprietary information, information such as client lists, marketing strategies, or software. Although these risks have always existed, employees now have greater opportunity to receive and transmit electronically inappropriate material such as pornography, or send mailing lists of clients to competitors. For these reasons and more, some major corporations such as Xerox have begun to routinely monitor their employees' behavior while making their policies known to their employees. "Productivity suffers when employees surf the Web on company time. Additionally, employers can face liability issues when employees access pornographic or inappropriate Web sites that may offend their colleagues," said Ellen Bayer, AMA's global practice leader on human resource issues.[3]

3. Ibid.

Privacy advocates and organizations such as the American Civil Liberties Union (ACLU), however, contend that the continued erosion of the employee's privacy in the workplace is growing unchecked. As the distinction between work and home blurs with more flexible work arrangements such as job sharing and telecommuting, the conflict between the employer's right to know what his employees are doing and the employee's right to maintain his right to privacy has sharpened. There are interesting questions that remain to be answered by new litigation or legislation. If, for example, the employee is using a home computer to do company work, should the company have unlimited access to the employee's machine?

The ACLU points to the paucity of laws protecting a worker's privacy as one of the major privacy issues. The Constitution simply does not apply to workers' rights. It was drafted in the eighteenth century to protect individual rights against government intrusion, but it could not have foreseen the advances in today's technology and the threat it poses to the office worker. Private sector employees in particular are vulnerable because most are not unionized and can be fired on the spot with little justification. The ACLU and other organizations feel that one reason many companies monitor their employees is not to protect the stockholders but to gather additional evidence against unwanted employees.[4]

What Are Employers Doing?

Advances in technologies have brought advances in surveillance and monitoring of employees' behavior in the work place. Unless

4. http:///www.aclu.org/issues/worker/iswr.html.

a company specifically states in a privacy policy that it does not monitor what its employees do on the job, an employee could safely assume that their company is performing some kind of surveillance activities, even if they are random "spot checks." In general, the kind of activities companies engage in include:

- Telephone monitoring

- Monitoring of electronic mail

- Computer monitoring

There are other aspects of nonelectronic monitoring of employees such as drug testing, credit checks, video cameras, and inquiries into an employee's medical history, but they are outside the scope of this book, which primarily focuses on how the tools an employee uses on the job can, in one sense, be used against him.

Telephone Monitoring

Under the 1986 Electronic Communications Privacy Act, more commonly known as the Federal Wiretap Act, penalties and civil damages can be exacted on a third party that intercepts a phone conversation without the consent of both parties participating in the conversation. Title 18 of the Omnibus Control and Safe Streets Act prohibits any individual or organization, including corporations, from intercepting electronic communications of others. This includes employers who may not monitor employee phone calls or e-mail when employees believe their communications are private (the exception to this rule is when the company has notified its employees in advance of its policy of monitoring employee communications to protect the company's interests). However, it is common practice for many corporations to listen in, particularly those in the service industry such as credit card companies that monitor employee calls for reasons of quality control.

Federal law does prohibit companies from listening in on personal calls, and the Omnibus Act prohibits a company's knowing disclosure of phone conversations to third parties. But if a company has a stated policy that an employee is not to use business phones for personal calls, the employee risks being overheard if he ignores the policy. Furthermore, employers may use devices called "pen registers" to record not only what phone numbers an employee calls, but also the length of each call, in order to determine how much time an employee spends on the phone for personal reasons.

The best course of action for employers who feel the need for and see the justification in monitoring calls is to state clearly their policy to their employees in order to reduce their expectations about how much privacy they have while on the phone. Employers should also ensure that they have an explicit business purpose for listening in, such as the monitoring of customer calls for quality control purposes (in fact, many companies who practice this will play a prerecorded message to alert both parties that the call may be monitored or recorded). If intrusive phone monitoring policies are in place, employers should make private phone lines or pay phones available to their employees for personal use.

Still, until a clearer set of laws governing the monitoring of employee phone calls are passed (and this may never happen), legal experts advise the employer to refrain from listening in unless it has an absolute business justification for doing so.

Monitoring E-Mail

The Fourth Amendment proscribes against unreasonable searches and seizures, but the law does not apply to the private workplace. Again, the point at which the employer's right to protect itself from theft and litigation ends and an employee's right to privacy begins is largely untested by the courts. For example, does a company have the absolute right to read employee e-mails if it is concerned about trade-secret violations, or is it reasonable for the employee to expect that the contents of his e-mail are private? Does a company have the right to monitor the Web sites an employee visits on the suspicion that the employee is disseminating pornographic material and inviting a harassment lawsuit, or does the employee have a reasonable expectation that his every move is not being watched?

Employers argue that because they own the employee's computer and the network that it runs on, they also own the contents of the computer and have a right to inspect how it is being used. Employees, however, argue that they do not surrender their civil liberties when they enter the office at 9:00 A.M. and pick them up again when they leave at 5:00 P.M.

Court cases are pending in which an employee's right to privacy when using electronic mail is being tested. However, current practices allow the company in most cases to review the contents of e-mail. If the employer has no stated policy regarding this practice, the employee has no way of knowing if his mail is being read. The employer that does publish its policy to its employees is legally bound to abide by it. Even then, the employee is unable to detect when an unintended party is reading his mail or when his surfing on the Internet is being tracked.

Once again, legal experts warn companies against engaging

in reading employee e-mail unless they have a strong business justification for doing so. A clear and concise policy communicated by memo, in the employee handbook, or in a union contract will help the employee understand the limits placed on the usage of e-mail until such time as the courts rule more definitively on the issue.

Monitoring the Computer

Consider this scenario. An employee is searching the Internet for information related to a project that requires background research. During his lunch break, the employee decides to visit his favorite online bookseller to do a little browsing, and then goes to a national news service to read an in-depth article about a snippet of news he heard on the radio while driving to work. A few days later, his manager calls him in the office to warn him about visiting personal Web sites on company time and puts him on probation.

In another department, a data entry clerk receives a poor review after his manager tells him that he isn't typing fast enough and his expected output is below service level agreements promised to the customer. He is also spending too much time organizing a family reunion on company time.

Yet another employee is demoted because her computer, her manager tells her, is idle more often than not. If the employee isn't using the computer, then she must be doing something unrelated to company business.

This is not science fiction. Employers today have a number of software tools available to them to record most aspects of employees' behavior on the computer. Keystroke monitoring, for example, is a practice whereby employers (or husbands, or wives, or parents) use a software tool to silently monitor all computer activity.

The Department of Justice (DOJ) has used keystroke monitoring for a number of years to detect intruders who access government systems without authority or with insufficient authority. Even though the DOJ does not authorize keystroke monitoring— not even implicitly—there remain few laws to prevent an organization from tracking what its employees enter on their computers.

This situation is further complicated by a number of software tools that make the job of keystroke monitoring easy and invisible, tools such as KeyKey, Keyloggers, and WinWhatWhere.

WinWhatWhere, for example, allows the user to track not only what an individual types, but also the day and time he types it, and can log this information for review in a configurable report (see Figure 3-2).

Furthermore, many of these tools can store the information in compressed format and send it to a predesignated address. Such tools are designed ostensibly for use by law enforcement and government agencies to investigate criminal activity, but there's little to prevent a private company from using a keystroke monitor to keep tabs on its employees, especially since so many of the good ones are available for free.

Other tools make it possible to record what is on a user's screen or stored on his hard drive. One such tool, Spector, records PC and Internet activity and plays back the recorded information. Spector tracks applications that are loaded, Web sites that are visited, conversations conducted in chat rooms, keystrokes typed (even if they are deleted before the document is saved), and e-mail

Figure 3-2 Detail of WinWhatWhere's Keystroke Capture

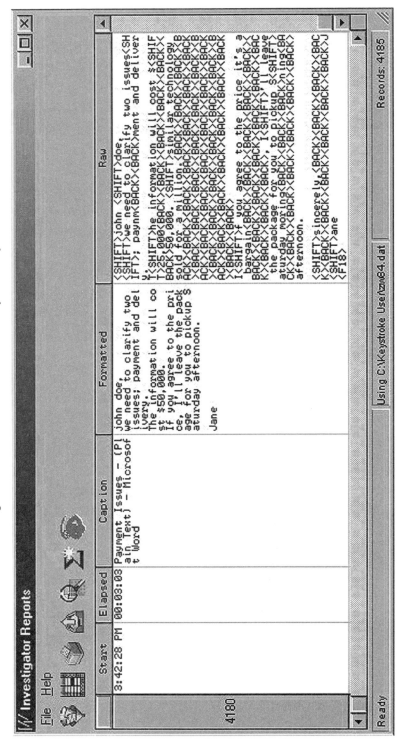

Reprinted with permission of WinWhatWhere Corporation. http://www.winwhatwhere.com.

Figure 3-3   Spector Casts a Long Shadow

Reprinted with permission of SpectorSoft Corporation. http://www.spectorsoft. com.

that is sent and received. Spector bills the tool as ideal for wives who want to trap cheating spouses, parents who want to know what their children are doing on the computer, or employers who want to track their employees (see Figure 3-3).

Although state laws vary—California being one of the most active states in issues involving employee rights in the workplace—employers generally may use software tools to monitor their employees' work habits provided they have clearly outlined their policies to their employees and can make a good case for their actions. Given this classic standoff between management and labor, what can both parties do to protect themselves?

"Do's" and "Don'ts"

So what should company managers do to safely walk the thin line between liberty and tyranny?

Management "Can Do's"

Perhaps the most important principle that a company can follow in regards to privacy in the electronic workplace is to publicize its intentions to their employees. The more upfront an organization is with its employees by spelling out its practices, the better their employees will understand the constraints under which they work. Policies regarding e-mail, phone mail, and use of the Internet should be easy to understand and highly visible. They should be disseminated in a way that employees could not possibly miss them, whether distributed through face-to-face training, company Web sites, employee handbooks, corporate e-mails, etc. This may not be the palliative that privacy advocates are looking for, but until legislation is enacted (if it is ever enacted) that clearly defines the privacy rights of employees in the workplace, forewarned is forearmed.

There are other steps an organization can take to avoid employee complaints and lawsuits. Rather than simply write policy, some companies are using tools to enforce policy. Rather than simply putting out the fire, some companies are trying to take away the matches by using filtering solutions to manage and monitor employee use of the Internet. One marketer of proxy filters, Websense, Inc., integrates its enterprise solution with an organization's proxy servers, firewalls, or as a stand-alone proxy server (see Figure 3-4).

Figure 3-4   Websense Enterprise Solution

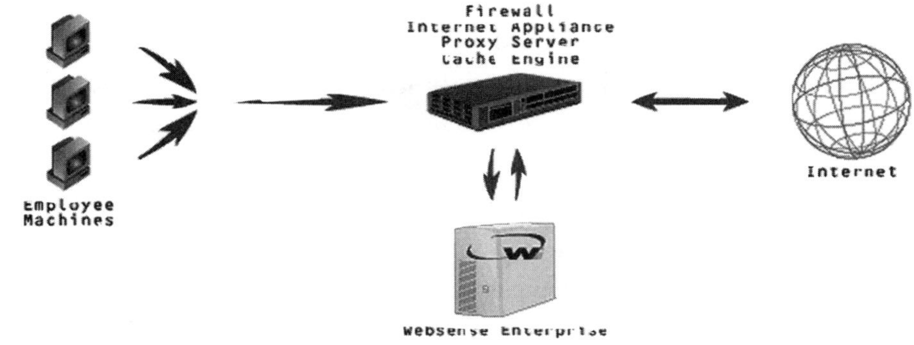

Reprinted with permission of Websense, Inc.

Websense includes a "master database" that contains the addresses of more than 1.4 million sites that a company probably doesn't want its employees to visit, organized into multiple categories including shopping, adult content, gambling, and MP3 sites. According to Websense, their database is constantly updated using artificial intelligence and "Internet Analysts."

Other proxy filters such as Microsoft and Netscape's Proxy Servers and Novell's BorderManager work in much the same way. They assist companies with managing how the Internet is used, securing the network environment, and lowering costs by controlling bandwidth. Considering that Internet access in the workplace is becoming widespread, proxy filters could be a useful tool for keeping employees out of trouble.

Employee "Can Do's"

The prudent employee would be wise to understand his employer's policies regarding the use of phone, fax, e-mail, the Internet, etc., and, if the employer doesn't have a stated policy, to ask his human resource department or ombudsperson. Common sense seems to dictate that an employee would refrain from visiting adult content sites on the Internet during work hours, exchanging offensive e-mail, or otherwise engage in behavior that is unbecoming or unprofessional, let alone illegal. Unfortunately, whether out of sheer boredom or an inadequate upbringing or criminal intent, some employees will continue to ignore company guidelines and raise the privacy issue in the workplace.

If an employee does have a complaint with his organization's privacy policy and feels the response he gets is inadequate, he can also contact his federal legislators, in particular members of the House and Senate Labor committees. Outside of government agencies, several private organizations such as the ACLU's National Task Force on Civil Liberties in the Workplace or the Electronic Messaging Association advocate stronger government regulation of employee monitoring activities and may be able to give assistance.[5]

Is Federal Action Required?

As of this writing, Congress is considering legislation introduced in both Houses that would require companies to inform employees if they monitor their use of the telephone, e-mail, and their computer. The law, introduced by Senator Charles Schumer, a Democrat from New York, would mandate employers tell their employees once a year how they are watching and what they are doing with the information they gather if they are

5. http://www.privacyrights.org/fs/fs7-work.htm.

watching. If an employee discovered that he was being watched without being notified, he could sue his employer for up to $20,000.[6] "We're not saying 'abolish this practice,' we're just saying employees have a right to know when they're being watched," said Schumer.

Schumer expects the bill to pass considering its light-handedness. Still, privacy advocates are likely to push for greater protections in the work place. Lew Malthby, president of the National Workrights Institute, says that the "vast majority" of employers makes some statement to their employees that they are being watched, but according to Malthby the statements are usually vague and give the employee no real idea of how they are being monitored. ACLU legislative counsel Greg Nojeim feels that these kinds of "blanket statements" would not be specific enough to satisfy the intent of the bill should it pass. Passage of the bill could force employers to be more upfront about how they collect data about their employees and what they do with the data.

Big Brother Is Seemingly Alive and Well

In Letter VI of Panopticon, Bentham concludes:

> In no instance could his [the "keeper's"] subordinates either perform or depart from their duty, but he must know the time and degree and manner of their doing so. . . . It is this circumstance that renders the influence of this plan not less beneficial to what is called liberty, than

6. http://www.thestandard.com/article/display/0,1151,17026,00.html.

to necessary coercion; not less powerful as a control [sic] upon subordinate power, than as a curb to delinquency; as a shield to innocence, than as a scourge to guilt.[7]

What Bentham could not have foreseen was the far-reaching consequences of almost unrestricted electronic surveillance in the workplace. The keeper is now the system security administrator who has the tools to monitor virtually anything an employee does in the workplace. It is clear that federal legislation will be required to minimally force employers to specifically state their monitoring and surveillance policies and make them known to their employees.

Speaking of federal regulation, let's now take a look to see where U.S. and international laws are headed to deliver an end to privacy abuses on the Internet.

7. Jeremy Bentham, "Panopticon," from *Writing and Reading Across the Curriculum*, Laurence Behrens and Leonard Rosen, eds. (New York: Longman, 6th ed., 1997).

Privacy Knows
No Borders

Buried deep in the preamble of the European Union's Data Protection Policy, is a seemingly innocuous "Whereas" in a sea of "whereases" (72 to be exact) that reads:

> "[Clause] 57. Whereas, on the other hand, the transfer of personal data to a third country which does not ensure an adequate level of protection must be prohibited."

It's not often that Americans think of the United States as a "third country," but the Europeans certainly do see the United States as an outsider. The United States has been at odds with the members of the European Union (EU) over its privacy policies since they were created.

The European Directive on Privacy Policy

The EU directive, drafted in 1995 and made into law in October 1998, spells out to the member states of the EU, and to those outside it who wish to do business with them, the policies and procedures for the collection, use, and transfer of personal data across borders, including the transport of data to non-EU ("third") countries.

Article 25 of the EU directive elaborates on the meaning of Clause 57 and in doing so has caused great consternation in the United States:[1] Specifically, Article 25 states that:

1.   *A Member State can transfer personal data to a "third county" (i.e., a country outside the EU) for further processing only if that country ensures an "adequate level of protection."* Unless a country outside the EU can prove that it "adequately" protects the data that it receives from outside its borders, a Member State may not transmit personal data to that country (see paragraph 2 below for the Commission's definition of "adequate"). Article 2 loosely defines "personal data" as "any information relating to an identified or identifiable natural person ('data subject'); an identifiable person is one who can be identified, directly or indirectly, in particular by reference to an identification number or to one or more factors specific to his physical, physiological, mental, economic, cultural or social identity." One could safely assume with this broad interpretation that "personal data" would include:

- Social security number

- Birth date and place of birth

1. http://www.cdt.org/privacy/eudirective/EU_Directive_.html#HD_NM_45.

- Mental and physical health records

- Borrowing habits at the public library

- Affiliations with political organizations, etc.

2.   *The Directive specifically excludes two categories of personal data from its purview: that which applies to government and therefore sovereign activities, and personal data related to public or state security and defense. This "level of protection" will be assessed based on the nature of the data, how it will be used, to whom the data might be transferred (if anyone), how long it will be retained, etc., and the "rules of the law" in force including security measures.* The EU will consider a number of factors including government policy and regulations ("rules of the law") of the "third country" as well as security policies and procedures of the recipient when determining what "level of protection" is required. For example, if the data being transmitted to a third country does not contain personally identifying information, the level of protection needed would be less than if the data were to contain employee confidential information such as birth dates or social security numbers.

3.   *Member States and the Commission will alert each other in cases where they believe a third country is not complying with EU data protection policies.* Member states and the Commission are required to notify each other any breaches of the EU directive, including identifying third countries failing to comply with the guidelines of the directive.

4.   *If the Commission determines that a third country is not providing an adequate level of protection, Member States will desist from transferring similar* data to the third country. The Commission forbids Member States from transmitting data to

third countries that don't meet the requirements for privacy protection in accordance with Article 31 of the directive. A committee composed of representatives of the Member States and headed by a representative of the Commission will assist the Commission. This committee will render its opinion and, if required, Member States will desist from transmitting data of the same type to the third country in question.

5. *The Commission will investigate and negotiate a solution to such an infraction as described above (#4).* The Commission in accordance with the provisions of Paragraph 4 will investigate the reported infraction and propose a remedy, if required.

6. *The Commission may determine that a third country may already have domestic laws sufficient to protect "private lives" as well as through existing international commitments.* The Commission may find that a third country already has adequate national and international laws and agreements that obviate any restrictions on the transmission of data.

At stake is the United State's ability (as well as the ability of other non-EU states) to transmit personally identifying information from one of the member EU states. This has serious implications about the ability of U.S. companies to operate in Europe. Companies could be prevented from transferring records of employees of an international subsidiary to the home office in the United States. This directive has profound implications not only for the growth of international electronic commerce in Europe, but also for privacy policy in the United States in which corporations and privacy advocates lobby for their causes.

At issue is whether or not the European data protection laws will become the global privacy standard. Congress is becoming increasingly worried that such an event could have dire implications for U.S. businesses, costing corporations hundreds of thousands of dollars to develop processes that, for example, would allow consumers to access their data. However, some Congressional members such as Representative Edward J. Markley (D.-Mass.) back the European privacy directive, stating that most Americans favor strong privacy rules similar to those in Europe.[2]

Representative Steve Buyer (R.-Ind.) counters that Americans want less government intrusion, not more. Thus the issue of privacy involves fundamentals of American history and diplomacy that pit individual freedoms against government control, consumer rights against *laissez-faire* economic policy, national economic interests against a global economy.

The debates between the EU and the U.S. Department of Commerce heated up in October 1998 when the EU Data Directive Policy took effect. Essentially the directive requires EU members to enact laws regulating how they process personal data within the European Union and to enforce those laws. The scope of the directive is expanded in Article 25 by requiring that personal information may be sent to countries outside the EU only if those countries can guarantee an adequate level of protection for the "subject" of the data. The ultimatum is, third countries such as the United States, whose privacy practices are not deemed adequate by the EU Commission, will *not be allowed* to process and transfer personal data collected in one of the EU states.

The ramifications of the EU's privacy policy for U.S. business interests are enormous. They affect every industry from manufacturing and medical services to the financial services industries. Unless companies in third countries can show that they have

2. www.techlawjournal.com/privacy/199904076.htm.

taken adequate steps to protect data subjects, they will not be allowed to collect, process, and disseminate data about EU subjects, including foreign-based employees of American corporations. Data that may be restricted include:

- Date of birth

- Number or names of dependents

- Name of spouse

- Place of residence

- Medical insurance elections

- Salary history and amounts, taxes paid, etc.

- Data required to maintain employment records

OECD Sets the Precedent

The EU directive is not the first effort to codify a set of privacy principles controlling the flow of data across national boundaries. The Organization for Economic Cooperation and Development (OECD), a member group of thirty "like-minded" countries (some of the larger economies include Canada, France, Germany, Italy, Japan, Spain, the United Kingdom and the United States) who collectively produce two thirds of the world's goods and services,[3] has grappled with the issue since the 1970s. Sometimes dubbed a "rich man's club" or "think tank," the OECD defines itself as "a setting in which to discuss, develop and perfect economic

3. http://www.oecd.org.

and social policy. . . [to] compare experiences, seek answers to common problems and work to co-ordinate domestic and international policies that increasingly in today's globalised world must form a web of even practice across nations."[4] It is, in effect, a collection of committees whose overseer is the Council, which is composed of one representative from each of the member states. Members of the organization are funded by their countries, but although they serve as professional civil servants they have no traditional affiliation with their respective countries. The Council meets at the ministerial level once a year, gives public prominence to important issues such as the need to crack down on bribery or end subsidies to shipbuilders, resulting more often than not in informal discussions that show the impact of national policies on the international community.

In September 1980, the OECD adopted a set of guidelines concerning the protection of privacy and the flow of data across national borders. The authors of the guideline developed a broad set of principles they felt would help "harmonize" national privacy legislations and protect privacy rights without interrupting the international flow of data. These guidelines have since become the foundation for most of the current self-regulatory, national, and international laws including the EU directive.

The guidelines were set forth as voluntary principles, and by 1980 almost half of the OECD member nations had passed or begun work on developing their own privacy policies. By 1983 the OECD reported that almost 200 U.S. companies claimed to have agreed with the spirit of the guidelines although few had actually taken positive steps to implement them. The OECD guidelines contain eight principles:

4. Ibid.

1. Collection Limitation. Only that data pertaining to an individual that is necessary should be collected in a fair and lawful manner and with the consent of the data subject when appropriate.

2. Data Quality. Personal data should be relevant (i.e., not extraneous to the intended purpose), accurate, and up to date.

3. Purpose Specification. The collector should state the purpose of the personal data gathering no later than the time it is collected, and subsequent use should be in keeping with the stated uses.

4. Use Limitation. Personal data should be used only for the expressed purposes and should not be made available to a third party unless the data subject has consented or law allows it.

5. Security Safeguards. Personal data should be safe and secure from unlawful or inappropriate access. This includes the loss, modification, use, destruction, or disclosure of the data.

6. Openness. The general policies and procedures related to personal data should be open, meaning that the data subjects should know how their data is collected, how it is used, and who uses it, and be able to verify that the data exists.

7. Individual Participation. An individual should be able to verify whether or not data about him is being collected and, if so, he should be able to access the data in a reasonable manner. The individual should also be able to question the integrity of the data and add, modify, or delete the data.

8. Accountability. A data controller should be responsible for complying with the aforementioned principles.

The United States endorsed the OECD guidelines, underscoring the difference between endorsement and enforcement (i.e., the United States accepted the spirit of the OECD guidelines without actually enforcing them).

The OECD guidelines, although written before the Internet took data communications to a higher plane, presaged the growing importance of computer networks and the world economy, and served as a blueprint for the EU directive. They anticipated an increasingly complex global economy accelerated by technological advances that few could have foreseen.

U.S. Privacy Policy as Precedent

As the OECD guidelines helped form the EU directive, U.S. privacy policies laid the groundwork for the opposition. The United States has a patchwork approach to privacy that critics of self-regulation call "sector specific." A particular industry may support legislation that protects its "self" and its relationships, although the laws have no substantial meaning beyond the industry in question and don't result in comprehensive protection for individual consumers. Some examples of industry-specific legislation:

• The Video Privacy Protection Act of 1988 prevents a video tape service provider from disclosing to a third party personally identifying information about a customer, in this case the videos that a customer has rented. Interestingly this law was enacted after a reporter investigated Supreme Court nominee Judge Robert Bork's viewing tastes in 1987.

• The Right Financial Privacy Act protects the consumer from unlawful dissemination of personal financial information without the appropriate written authority.

• The Privacy Act of 1974 states that information collected for one purpose, for example income tax liability, cannot be used for other purposes or transferred to a third party, while protecting individual privacy rights is limited in scope.

Critics of the U.S. approach to privacy protection contend that these laws have little if any meaning beyond the industries for which they are intended, and they do not amount to a comprehensive and consistent privacy policy. Although it's comforting to know that our rental records at Blockbuster Video are no longer public domain, the Video Privacy Protection Act does nothing to stop an unscrupulous Web site from selling personal data to an Internet marketing firm.

The Gathering Storm Clouds

In October of 1998, the EU Data Protection Directive became law after three years of negotiation, causing officials in the U.S. Department of Commerce to scramble.

The passage of the directive underscored the ongoing battle in the United States between those favoring self-regulation, typically major corporations such as Microsoft and IBM who have much at stake in the global marketplace, and privacy advocates who feel that the industry is unwilling or unable to safeguard adequately personally identifying information. "The directive has raised the visibility of privacy law in the U.S.," said Peter Swire, law professor at Ohio State University and coauthor of *None of Your Business: World Data Flows, Electronic Commerce, and the European Privacy Directive.* "Some of the least defensible corporate practices in the U.S. are coming under pressure," he added.[5]

The problem, according to Swire, was the European stance that the United States had no consistent and enforceable privacy standard in the private sector. Although the U.S. federal government is careful to protect its own systems from being compromised, it has a spotty record when it comes to passing laws that protect private citizens, and it is the individual that is the intended target of the EU directive. Though the EU understood that crossing the line into international policy was not only unfeasible but dangerous as well, and doing so could be viewed as protectionist and create antagonism between itself and third countries, it passed the policy anyway.

The EU contends that the directive is not an attempt to dictate its own privacy policies to the rest of the world, but a natural progression in the consolidation and unification of European economies since the end of World War II. To further this cause, they feel they had to address the issue of the different ways in which member states, and those outside the states, handle personal data, largely in response to the formation of the EU and the rapid advance of technology.

Thus the battle line was drawn between the EU member countries, whose directive attempts to protect its citizens without throttling international commerce, and the Department of Commerce and the powerful corporations that it represents. No one, including the EU, wanted to see the business flow from the United States dry up. Since the EU had no intention of backing off

5. http://www.nytimes.com/library/tech/98/10/cyber/cyberlaw/09law.html.

its directive, the spotlight turned on U.S. privacy policy and the debate within the United States. Thus began a two-year period of negotiations between the United States and the EU culminating in an agreement that the two parties struck in July 2000.

The Safe Harbor Privacy Principles

The result of the negotiations between the U.S. Department of Commerce and the EU was The Safe Harbor Privacy Principles, a framework that allows U.S. organizations to meet the minimum requirements of the directive.[6] The Commission announced on July 27, 2000, that the Safe Harbor arrangement would satisfy the European directive's standards and thus allow the United States to continue processing and transmitting personal data outside the EU.

The Safe Harbor Privacy Principles are in accordance with Article 25.6 of the EU's directive in that they provide "adequate protection" of personal data. U.S. organizations may voluntarily enter into the Safe Harbor Agreement, thus making the approval of the EU member states automatic.

To determine if a U.S. organization is a participant in the Safe Harbor Agreement, an EU organization may view a list of safe harbor organizations on a Web site (i.e., www.ita.doc.gov/ecom) maintained by the U.S. Department of Commerce, a list that became available in November 2000.

The agreement surprised those who followed the European Commission's negotiations with the United States because of the Commission's skepticism of the former's ability to self-regulate.

6. http://www.ita.doc.gov/td/ecom/SafeHarborOverviewAug00.htm.

However, the EU member states unanimously passed the Safe Harbor Privacy Principles with the proviso that the Commission would watch closely regulatory developments in the United States and request periodic reviews.

What Are the Safe Harbor Privacy Principles?

Four documents define the terms of the Safe Harbor[7]:

1. *The International Safe Harbor Principles.* Focus is on the privacy principles with which you're undoubtedly familiar by now:

- **Notice.** The company must notify individuals what personally identifying information it is collecting, why it is collecting it, how to contact the collector, any third parties to which it discloses personal information, and the means by which the individual can limit or cease the use of this information.

- **Choice.** Individuals must be able to choose whether and how their personal information is used by or disclosed to third parties.

- **Onward Transfer.** Third parties receiving the information are required by the company to provide the same level of privacy protection as the company itself.

7. http://www.ici.org/issues/eu_more1_privacy.html.

- **Security.** The company must secure the data and prevent the loss, misuse, disclosure, alteration, and unauthorized access of personal data.

- **Data Integrity.** Individuals must be reassured that their data is complete, accurate, current, and used for its intended purposes only.

- **Access.** Individuals must have the right and ability to access their personal data and view, correct, modify, or delete any portion of it.

- **Enforcement.** Each company must institute methods of enforcing the aforementioned privacy principles.

2. *FAQs, or Frequently Asked Questions.* Fifteen sets of FAQs elaborate on the safe harbor principles.

3. *Exchange of Letters.* Ambassador David Aaron of the Department of Commerce, in a letter to John Mogg of the European Commission, formally requests that the European Commission stipulate that those companies entering the Safe Harbor Principles have a "presumption of adequacy" that in effect provides a self-assessment of capability to meet the Safe Harbor requirements.

4. *Article 25.6 Decision on Adequacy.* Attached to John Mogg's letter to the U.S. Department of Commerce will be the Article 25.6 decision, which empowers the European Commission to determine that a third country is providing adequate data protection according to the terms of the directive.

How Does an Organization Sign Up?

An organization wishing to enter the Safe Harbor can do so voluntarily. The organization must comply with the International Safe Harbor Principles, declare so publicly, and self-certify annually with the Department of Commerce, stating in writing that it agrees to adhere to and enforce the Safe Harbor Principles. For an organization to qualify for the Safe Harbor and get added to the list of organizations that the Department of Commerce maintains, the organization must do at least one of the following:

1. Join a self-regulatory privacy program such as a seal program that adheres to the safe harbor principles.

2. Create its own self-regulatory privacy policy.

3. Be subject to a regulatory, administrative, or statutory body of law that has the same effect as a self-regulatory privacy program.

Thus, the emphasis of the Safe Harbor agreement is on self-regulation, not governmental legislation—a move that reassured opponents of government interference while dismaying privacy advocates.

How Will the Safe Harbor Be Enforced and Where?

The enforcement of the Safe Harbor in the United States will be conducted primarily in the private sector, the targeted audience of the directive. However, self-regulation in the private sector will be backed up by government enforcement of fair and protective statutes at the state and federal levels. The private sector, as part of the self-regulatory principles, must institute a method of resolving disputes and individual complaints, and must be able to verify compliance. This could happen in part or in whole through a privacy seal program. Failure on the part of a member organization to abide by the Safe Harbor Principles could result in action by the state and/or federal government. The FTC, for example, could impose an injunction and civil penalties of up to $11,000 per day on a company that has entered into the Safe Harbor agreement.

Is Everybody Happy?

The Department of Commerce and the European Commission hailed the Safe Harbor Principles as a consistent and affordable means of allowing third countries to continue transferring data outside the European Union. "It removes a thorn in the side of U.S.-EU trade relations. To get this issue behind us is nothing but a good thing," said Robert Litan, director of economic studies at the Brookings Institution.[8] IBM saw it as a model for other issues related to the transfer of data and privacy and a significant political accomplishment.

However, privacy advocates such as Marc Rotenberg, executive director of the Electronic Privacy Information Center (EPIC) in Washington, stated that while the Safe Harbor appeared to resolve the problem of relations between the United States and the European states, it raised the issue of whether U.S. organizations will safeguard European personal information more carefully than that of its own citizens. "There's a real issue

8. http://washingtonpost.com/wp-dyn/articles/A41418-2000Jun1.html.

of how this thing is going to be enforced," Rotenberg concluded.[9] Privacy advocates worry that the agreement will stall
further debate in the United States for privacy legislation.

Furthermore, several major U.S. corporations such as
General Electric Co., Visa USA, and Home Depot Inc. worry that
the Safe Harbor agreement burdens U.S. companies by requiring
more stringent protections than are required in their own country. The National Business Coalition on E-Commerce and Privacy
stated in a letter to David Aaron that the "EU privacy principles
that would be effectively imposed on American business by this
agreement far exceed any privacy requirements that have ever before been imposed in the United States."[10] Still, the National
Business Coalition stated that it will attempt to make the Safe
Harbor work to avoid a complete shutdown of the flow of data
from the European Union. The question is, can this be done effectively and meaningfully?

The Policy Heard 'Round the World

Certainly the United States is not the only third country affected
by the EU directive, specifically Article 25. Any non-EU member
state that attempts the transfer of data outside the EU is affected.
But how much a particular country is affected depends upon the
state of that country's national privacy policies and how closely
they are consistent with the directive. As of this writing, both
Switzerland and Hungary were considered to have data protection
laws that broadly follow the guidelines of the EU directive, and

9. Ibid.
10. Ibid.

other countries such as Australia, Canada, and Japan have already begun discussions with the EU. Australia, for example, has a Federal Privacy Commissioner, Malcolm Crompton, who has begun debate in that country over the handling of personal data. Canada enacted on 1 January 2001, the Personal Information Protection and Electronic Documents Act that establishes rules governing the collection, use, and disclosure of personal information in the private sector.

Privacy concerns are universal. How successful the directive and the Safe Harbor Principles will be in protecting privacy remains to be seen.

What is certain is that privacy concerns—and controls to assuage those concerns—are being mandated, and governments worldwide won't rest on the sidelines hoping the industry will come to its senses on its own.

The Imperative of
Privacy Policies

As public awareness of technology grows, so does its concern over the threat that automation poses to privacy. This fear is not just media hype. Survey results such as those gathered by the Pew Internet and American Life Project give the dimensions of how real public concern is.

In an August 2000 survey conducted by the Pew Internet and American Life Project (www.pewInternet.org) about trust and online privacy, two concerns of online users became clear. First, "Online Americans" (as the survey calls them) are concerned about their privacy to the point that they take it for granted. Second, these users do not understand how their behaviors are observed, and they don't know how to protect themselves from unwarranted intrusions into their lives. Fears run strongest among first-time users, parents, and women who feel particularly vulnerable in the online world.

According to the study, the bigger fears concerning privacy are:

• The risk of businesses and strangers obtaining their personal information (84 percent).

• Using their credit cards to complete an online transaction (68 percent).

• The risk of identity theft (68 percent).

• The transmission and mishandling of medical information online (54 percent).

• Contracting a computer virus when downloading a file (54 percent).

It is particularly startling that these same users presume that their personal information is safe, and that they have to "opt in" (in other words, give permission to the Internet site) before the site can collect the information. They have no idea that the FTC and a number of Web advertisers actually require users to specify that they don't want their personal data to be used. This method is known as the "opt out" method.

The survey also indicates that the majority of online users say they want to know the specifics of a site's privacy policy although we currently have no statistics on exactly how many users actually read a Web site's privacy policy.

Users who sense that a site is concealing its privacy practices or determine that a site is not enforcing its privacy policy will avoid visiting the site again. Ninety-four percent of the survey respondents even said they felt that some form of discipline was needed for abusive sites. According to the survey, although users may not recognize all the "tricks" a site uses to harvest their personal data, they do know problems created by such practices, and they seek revenge.

Given the ongoing concern of the FTC toward stricter regulation, especially in the areas of children's online privacy and online profiling as evidenced in their reports to the U.S. Congress and workshops they conduct, organizations such as the United States Council for International Business (*www.uscib.org*) are urging companies to adopt their own privacy policies before the federal government does it for them. Privacy policies reassure users that sites understand the importance of safeguarding personal data. They are good for business because they give users the confidence to return to the site.

What Constitutes a Good Privacy Policy?

We can discuss the general framework of a working privacy policy, but we need to keep in mind that the following policy guidelines are general guidelines that will need to be tailored to each individual site. All policies should contain the same basic elements that are covered in the Safe Harbor Principles, and should answer specific questions. Following are some questions and sample policies:

Notice

The site should tell customers *what* personal information it collects and how it plans to use it.

• Is the actual identity of the user required, or are other personal characteristics sufficient?

• Does the site collect financial information such as credit card numbers to complete a transaction?

• What other system information about the user might be collected such as the domain name of the visitor, his e-mail address, user-specific information on the pages he visits, or other information that the user voluntarily supplies such as survey responses?

• Once collected, how is the information used? Is it used solely for internal review—for example, to monitor system performance—and then discarded?

• Is the information used to help improve Web content or to redesign page layout?

• Are user preferences stored?

• Of great concern to the customer: is the information transferred or sold to third parties for marketing purposes?

Notice Done Right

Figure 5-1 shows a condensed example of Yahoo!'s privacy policy from the *www.yahoo.com* Web site.

Consent

It is important to allow your customers to decide how their information will be used.

• Do you allow the customer to "opt out" of giving his e-mail address to other reputable organizations?

• Do you give the customer the ability to refuse receipt of mailings or announcements such as new product or service descriptions?

Figure 5-1   Yahoo!'s Privacy Policy

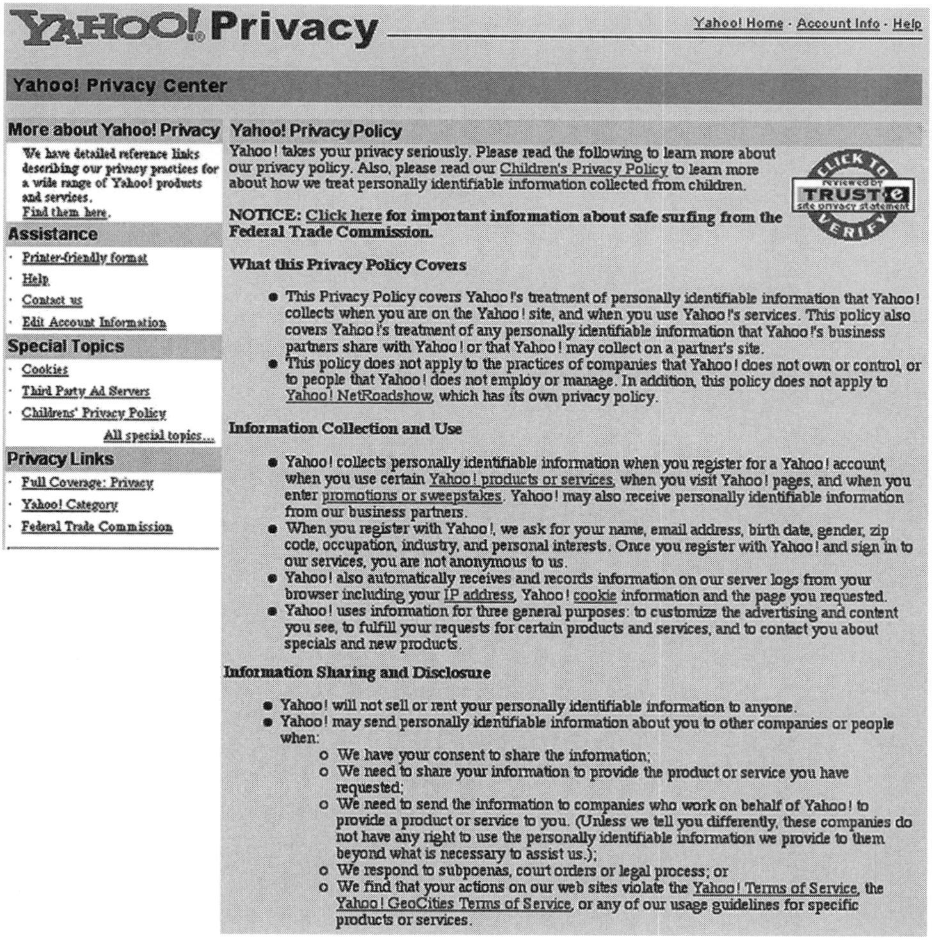

(continues)

Figure 5-1   (Continued)

Cookies

- Yahoo! may set and access Yahoo! cookies on your computer.
- Yahoo! allows other companies that are presenting advertisements on some of our pages to set and access their cookies on your computer. Other companies' use of their cookies is subject to their own privacy policies, not this one. Advertisers or other companies do not have access to Yahoo!'s cookies.
- Yahoo! uses web beacons to access our cookies within and outside our network of web sites and in connection with Yahoo! products and services.

Your Ability to Edit and Delete Your Account Information and Preferences

- Yahoo! gives you the ability to edit your Yahoo! Account Information and preferences at any time, including whether you want Yahoo! to contact you about specials and new products.
- You may request deletion of your Yahoo! account by visiting our Account Deletion page, verifying your password once more and confirming your choice to terminate the account. Please click here to read about what information may possibly remain in our archived records after your account has been deleted.

Security

- Your Yahoo! Account Information is password-protected for your privacy and security.
- In certain areas Yahoo! uses industry-standard SSL-encryption to protect data transmissions.

Changes to this Privacy Policy

- Yahoo! may amend this policy from time to time. If we make any substantial changes in the way we use your personal information we will notify you by posting a prominent announcement on our pages.

Questions or Suggestions

- If you have questions or suggestions complete a feedback form.
- Yahoo! is TRUSTe-certified. This certification applies to all English-language sites under the Yahoo.com domain. If you feel that your inquiry has not been satisfactorily addressed, you should contact TRUSTe, an independent privacy organization.

Reproduced with permission of Yahoo! Inc. © 2000 by Yahoo! Inc. YAHOO! and the YAHOO! logo are trademarks of Yahoo! Inc.

• Does the customer have control over how his telephone number is used, if supplied?

• Is he able to prevent any personal information from being divulged to a third party such as an online marketing firm that may collect information such as the customer's domain type, IP address, and clickstream information?

Consent Done Right

Figure 5-2 shows an example of how users of the Amazon.com Web site can set (or unset) their preferences for e-mail announce-

Figure 5-2   The Amazon.com Preference Selection Form

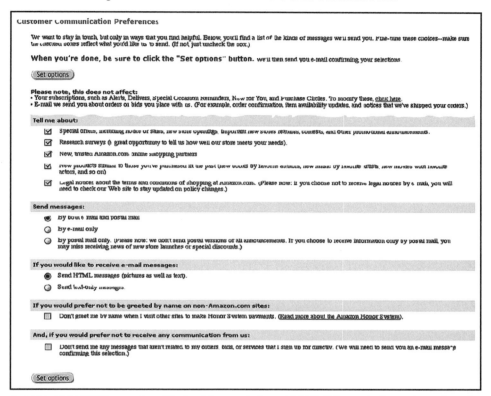

© 2001 AMAZON.com, Inc. Used with permission. AMAZON.com is the registered trademark of Amazon.com, Inc.

ments of products or services that interest them. Amazon provides high degrees of granular controls over information sharing.

Access

You should have a clear and recognizable process that allows the customer to review all information, including proprietary information, that you maintain about him.

Figure 5-3 Netscape Member Center Personal Information Maintenance Form

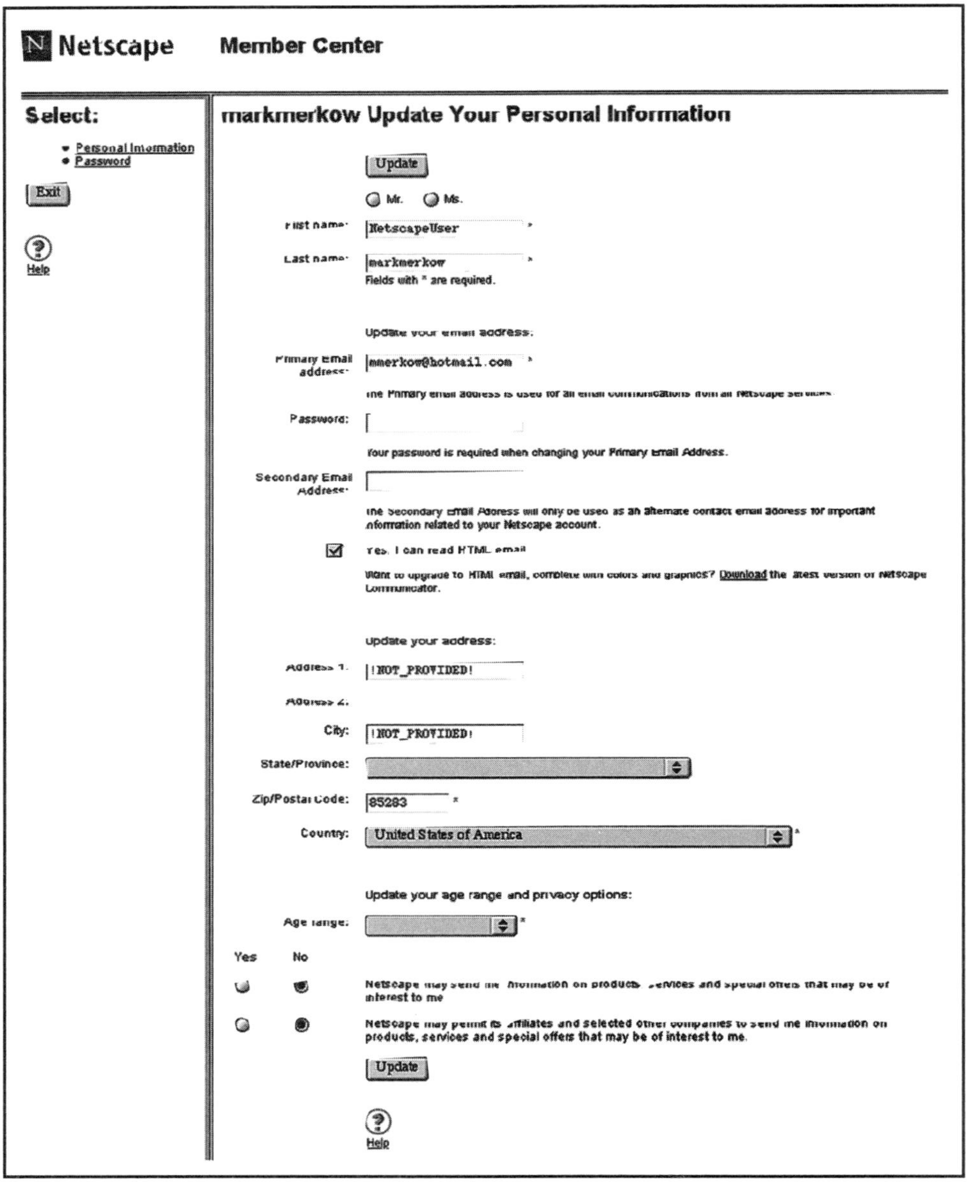

Screen shot used with permission. © 2001 Netscape. Commnications Corporation.

• Does this include financial information, customer identifiers, and passwords?

• Can the customer easily retrieve all transaction-related details such as items purchased, purchase dates, quantities, prices, etc.?

• Can the user track any inquiries or complaints he may have sent to your site?

• Of great concern to the customer: is he able to add, modify, or delete information that is incomplete or erroneous? If so, how does the customer contact you? By telephone (is your number clearly posted on the site?), by e-mail, by postal mail, or by visiting a secondary URL or using some other means? Is the method intuitive and easy to use?

• How quickly can the customer expect to have an inquiry or complaint resolved?

• How will he be contacted?

Access Done Right

Two examples of how access to stored information may be viewed and modified as desired are shown in Figures 5-3 and 5-4 from Netscape Communications and Yahoo!, respectively.

Security

You should have a clearly defined security policy and the measures to enforce it.

Figure 5-4   Yahoo! Account Information Maintenance Form

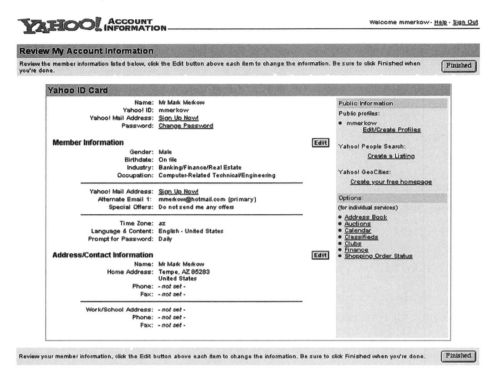

Reproduced with permission of Yahoo! Inc. © 2000 by Yahoo! Inc. YAHOO! and the YAHOO! logo are trademarks of Yahoo! Inc.

• Is personal data protected from loss, misuse, and alteration from both external and internal threats?

• Do you have contingency plans in place in case of hostile attacks?

• Does your site use industry-standard encryption when receiving and transferring customer data?

• Do you notify your customers that you are using strong-key encryption (such as SSL)?

• Is your physical site as well as your data secure from intruders?

• Do you backup data routinely to prevent accidental loss?

Security Done Right

Whereas many security countermeasures are invisible to all but those who intend harm to a Web site, some visible practices that consumers can take advantage of help to make the Web a safer place to shop and live.

American Express answers the concerns of those who are afraid or reluctant to share credit and charge card information via the Internet with the Private Payments system. It mitigates customer concern by generating a one-time, disposable credit card number that, even if compromised after transacting, is rendered useless. The Private Payments Web site is shown in Figure 5-5.

Figure 5-6 is one example of anonymous Web browsing services from Anonymizer.com, as one tool for consumers wishing to hide their identity while browsing the Internet.

The next three examples of security are implemented on the Arizona State University (ASU) Web site to help protect students from revealing private information unwillingly or unwittingly. Figure 5-7 shows the Warning Page that's displayed upon successful log-on to online services offered via the site. It instructs the user to pay close attention to navigation activities that could compromise personal security, especially on shared computer desktops.

Figure 5-8 highlights one feature of the ASU Web Online Student Schedule to help students further protect their identities when viewing grades or class schedule information. The arrow on

(text continues on page 98)

Figure 5-5 Private Payments from American Express

Figure 5-6   Anonymous Browsing Using Anonymizer

Reprinted with permission of Anonymizer, Inc. (http://www.anonymizer.com)

Figure 5-7   The ASU Web Warning Dialog Box

Reproduced with permission of ASU.

Figure 5-8   ASU Semester Schedule Selection Form

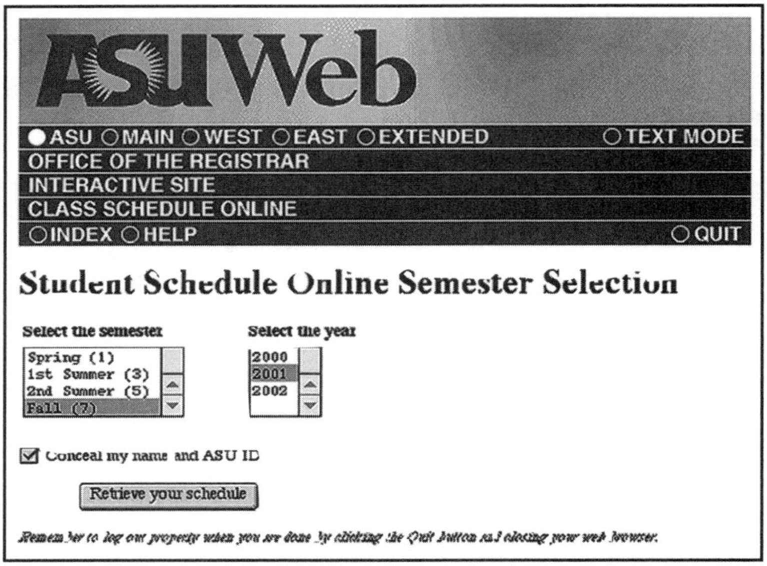

Reproduced with permission of ASU.

the diagram points to a check box to permit students to reveal their name and ID on the following page or not. Even if someone stands over the shoulder of a Web user, there's little fear that confidential or sensitive information will be compromised.

Figure 5-9 illustrates the effect on the ASU Class Schedule Form when the Reveal My Name and ASU ID check box is selected.

Enforcement

An essential part of your security policy should explain your enforcement policies to your customers.

Figure 5-9 Online Class Schedule with Privacy Features Selected

Arizona State University

Student Class Schedule
As of May 28, 2001, 8:22:55pm

(Name Concealed)   (ASU ID Concealed)   Spring 2001

Course	Line	Hours	Title	Audit	Time	Days	Bldg/Room	Instructor
M EDT		3.0	DEVEL COMPUTER BASED	N	4:40P	M		
Total Enrolled Hours		3.0						

Remember to log out properly when you are done by clicking the Quit button and closing your web browser.

Due to necessary nightly processing, the Interactive Web Site availability is limited to the following times:

Monday through Friday: 7 a.m. to 9 p.m.
Saturday: 7 a.m. to Noon
Sunday: Noon to 6 p.m.
The current Arizona date and time is **Mon May 28 20:22:56 2001**
All times listed are Mountain Standard Time. Arizona does not observe Daylight Savings Time.

Questions or comments? E-mail the Registrar's Office at registrar@asu.edu. Please note that e-mail is not secure and may be read by someone on the Internet. If you are uncomfortable with the possibility, please call us or write us with your request instead. Thank you!

The Office of the Registrar phone number is **(480) 965-3124.**

© 1997-2001 Arizona State University

Reproduced with permission of ASU.

• Are your policies reviewed periodically by a third party such as a seal program (e.g., TrustE, BBBOnLine)?

• If the customer feels your privacy policies are not being enforced, do you provide an address and/or phone number that he can contact to register a complaint?

• Do you provide the addresses of other organizations such as the Better Business Bureau, the state or local consumer protection office, or the Federal Trade Commission?

• Do you notify the customer that you have received the complaint and update him on the status of the complaint?

• Do you resolve complaints in a timely manner?

Children

If your site is directed at children under the age of 13, you will need to give special consideration to them when creating your privacy.

• Does your site comply with the Children's Online Privacy Protection Act (COPPA) that became law in April 2000? The law requires parental consent before a child may give personally identifying information on a site that the FTC deems is directed toward children (details of the law can be found at: www.ftc.gov/bcp/conline/pubs/buspubs/coppa.htm).

The Fair Operating Principles are generally considered to contain the standard elements of a privacy policy. Any privacy policy you adopt that contains these elements should reassure the customer that you are taking his personal data seriously. Keep in mind the following guidelines when creating your privacy policy:

- Make sure your policy is easy to read and find on your Web site (see the next section for advice on where to place your policy).

- Communicate to your own employees the importance of your privacy policy, especially to those who might have direct contact with the customer. Your employees should be able to respond to any concerns they receive from the customer.

- Consider your privacy policy a public relations tool as well as a safeguard for personal data. Companies with a privacy policy are going to be looked on more favorably by customers, lawmakers, and investors than those without a policy.

- Update your policy to reflect changes in your business and technology. Remember that change is the rule.

Where Do I Place My Privacy Policy?

Of course a privacy statement has little value if the customer can't find it. You must have a link to a notice of the site's privacy policy on your home page. It should be clear and prominently displayed. You might even want to consider requiring the Web page designer to use a larger font size or contrasting colors to accentuate the link. Figure 5-10 illustrates how the Travelocity.com Web site displays the link to the site's privacy policy.

If the home page is geared toward a general audience but has a link to a children's area, the site should have a link on each page, the first to the general privacy statement, and the second to the

Figure 5-10   Travelocity.com Home Page with Privacy Policy Link

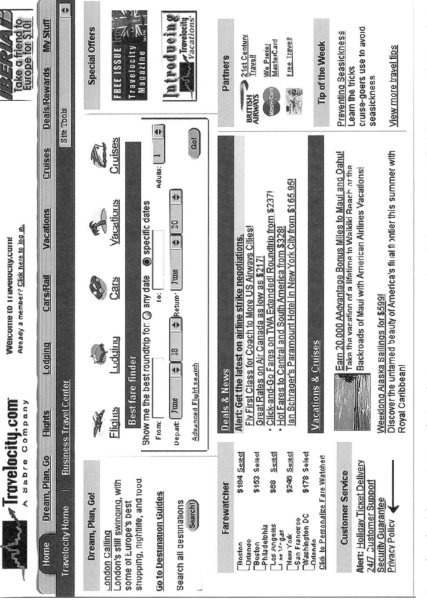

privacy statement for the children's area (note that a site can have more than one privacy policy based on the content of its pages).

How Do I Create My Privacy Policy?

Rising consumer concern over privacy matters has spawned a number of seal programs and consulting companies who are ready and willing to assist organizations in addressing privacy concerns. Services offered range from help with creating a privacy policy for a nominal fee to privacy audits and technology reviews that do not come cheaply. Yet another option is to keep your policy assessment in-house and "roll your own policy." The route that you take depends on the complexity of your site, the nature of your organization, the amount of personal data you collect and how you use it, in-house expertise, and, of course, your budget.

Creating your privacy policy in-house has some obvious advantages. First, the price tag is much lower because it doesn't involve using outside services. The main expense is the cost of finding the right expertise within your organization to develop the policy and put the mechanisms in place to enforce the policy, tasks that you would have to do anyway if you used an outside service. The main disadvantage, however, is the lack of a third-party endorsement by a recognizable entity such as the Better Business Bureau that reassures many consumers and regulatory agencies. Also, in-house privacy policies could weaken the case for self-regulation because they might lack the consistency and ubiquity of seal programs or other privacy platforms such as the P3P (discussed in Chapter 6).

Outsourcing the job of creating a privacy policy typically incurs greater expense than an in-house effort. A simple seal program, for example, only costs several hundred dollars with a nominal annual renewal fee, but a thorough audit of your procedures and policies by a "Big Five" accounting firm could cost thousands of dollars. The level of service you choose again depends upon the complexity of your site, the nature of your business, and the sophistication of your organization. Some organizations are also reluctant to "open their books" to an outside agency and feel they are putting themselves at risk by divulging organizational information to outsiders.

Despite these concerns, many organizations are turning to third-party seal programs or the use of other privacy tools for a number of reasons. First, by displaying a privacy seal of a trusted third party on its site, an organization can increase traffic through the reassurances the seal offers to the consumer. Knowing that the site uses an "industry standard" tool or seal program, the consumer has increased confidence that a respected privacy protection program is protecting his personal data. Second, by using a third party to create and monitor its privacy policy, an organization will be apprised of any changes in privacy law, both national and international, that it otherwise might miss through annual policy reviews. Finally, the consumer is reassured that if he does lodge a complaint against a site for violating its privacy policy, he knows that an "objective" third party will help mediate the case.

Given the advantages of using a third party to help create and monitor an organization's privacy policy, it's worth taking a look at some of the services that are currently being offered. A brief review of these services follows. Keep in mind that the list is not exhaustive but simply provides a range of services and prices as a general overview of what is available in the privacy marketplace.

Privacy Wizard

In April 2000, Microsoft, TRUSTe, and the Electronic Frontier Foundation announced a joint venture meant to help Web sites "fulfill their half of the privacy bargain."[1] The Privacy Wizard is a service that allows a company to answer a series of questions about the data it collects, how the company uses it, and how it protects the data. The Privacy Wizard generates a privacy statement once all the questions have been answered that can be downloaded to the company's site. Microsoft claims that completing the Privacy Wizard can take less than 30 minutes. The Privacy Wizard generates a boilerplate privacy statement and so includes a caveat that the statement will have to be tailored to the needs of the individual site after the initial policy is generated.

The Privacy Wizard is not a comprehensive approach to the privacy issue, but TRUSTe, a non-profit privacy seal program, and Microsoft call it a "good first step" toward developing a complete privacy program. The Privacy Wizard (www.truste.org/wizard), for example, asks questions about the kind of information collected such as contact information, financial information, personally identifying information, and any other information the site deems specific to the data subject. The Wizard also asks if the site uses cookies, the services of "advertising aggregators" (i.e., online marketing firms that collect user data such as personal preferences) such as DoubleClick, or if the site has links to third-party Web pages whose policies are not covered by the company's Web site. Questions also cover other important areas such as the use of public forums (e.g., chat rooms), data security, how it handles opt

1. http://www.wired.com/news/topstories/0,1287,18976,00.html.

in/out decisions, the kind of access the user has to personal information, and any children's guidelines that need to be considered.

Finally, the Privacy Wizard asks the user if he wants to become a TRUSTe licensee. Although a company may generate the privacy statement without signing up with TRUSTe, doing so does not allow it to display the TRUSTe trustmark on its site, and without the trustmark, TRUSTe claims that the consumer will not have the same level of confidence in your site.

To obtain the TRUSTe trustmark, a company must complete additional paperwork including submitting a final, edited version of its privacy policy along with a completed self-assessment form and a signed agreement that states that the company will pay TRUSTe an annual licensing fee. TRUSTe uses a sliding fee schedule based on the company's annual revenue, ranging from $299 per year for a company with less than $1 million in annual revenues to $6,999 for companies with over $75 million in annual revenues. The fee schedule is designed to allow small businesses as well as large corporations to afford the seal program while promoting the cause of self-regulation.

Direct Marketing Association

The Direct Marketing Association (DMA) is the oldest (organized in 1917) and largest trade association for users and suppliers in direct, data gathering, and computerized marketing, representing close to 5,000 commercial and not-for-profit member organizations. Recognizing the impact that e-commerce has had and will continue to have on marketing, DMA purchased the Association for Interactive Media (AIM) and the Internet Alliance, both trade associations with expertise in the fields of electronic marketing.

Among the many services DMA provides to consumer marketers, B2B marketers, and suppliers, it also offers members a sixteen-question privacy policy generator based on the DMA's Privacy Principles for Online Marketing that a company can download to its site (at no charge to the user). Questions cover the spate of privacy questions ranging from the kind of data that are collected to the uses to which it is put, how it is protected, the control users have over data collection and usage, the use of ad servers, etc.

As with the TrustE program, the DMA offers a reasonable first step toward creating a privacy policy. Unlike the Privacy Wizard, the DMA does not offer a trustmark along with the privacy policy statement that the user generates. However, the DMA does hold strict privacy standards for its member organizations that were codified in the October 1997 "Privacy Policy to American Consumers."[2] The DMA is yet another organization promoting self-regulation over increased government involvement in privacy matters.

PrivacyBot.com

PrivacyBot.com is a seal program that offers the "PrivacyBot Drafting System" for generating a privacy statement, the "PrivacyBot TrustMark," which a company can display on its site along with the generated policy statement, and the "PrivacyBot Mediation Service" that assists Web sites and consumers in resolving privacy complaints "without getting lawyers involved."[3]

2. http://www.the-dma.org/library/privacy/privacypromise.shtml.
3. http://www.privacybot.com/about.shtm.

The PrivacyBot.com organization is strong competition for the TRUSTe trustmark.

PrivacyBot.com generates an XML version of the user's privacy statement to be posted on a Web site to help implement the Platform for Privacy Preferences (discussed in Chapter 6), and a text version to be used for humans to read. PrivacyBot.com charges a nominal fee of $100 for a two-year membership in the PrivacyBot Registry, and charges an additional nominal fee for the use of its nonbinding online mediation service.

BBBOnLine.com

The BBBOnLine.com offers a seal program with the advantage of the Better Business Bureau's name recognition. Before a company applies for membership, it must complete and post a privacy policy statement. BBBOnLine.com differs from the other services available in that the statement is a prerequisite to enrollment, not a part of the process. Their site (www.BBBOnLine.com) offers guidance on how to create a privacy statement but does not offer a "wizard" to help you build it. Rather, the site offers a guideline that identifies the important information that should be in the statement.

With privacy statement in hand, the company needs to follow a five-step process to join the BBBOnLine seal program: (1) Complete an application and pay a one-time application fee of $75 and an annual assessment fee. The latter is a sliding fee schedule based on total company sales, both offline and online. The fee ranges from as little as $150 for companies with less than $1 million in sales revenue to $5,000 for companies with sales exceeding $2 billion. Once the application and fees are received, the company will be assigned a compliance analyst to evaluate the application. (2) Complete the Privacy Policy Assessment Questionnaire. The questionnaire asks the full range of questions about the data that is collected, how it is used, user access, etc. (3) Submit the questionnaire to a compliance analyst for review. (4) Once the compliance analyst has approved the application, the company must complete two signed copies of the "Participant License Agreement." (5) Install the BBBOnLine seal on your Web site (see Chapter 10).

USCIB

The USCIB was founded in 1945 to promote open global trade, investment, and finance. Its membership includes over 300 multinational companies and other legal and business organizations that collectively create policy statements and promote international trade through the "harmonization" of commercial practices (the USCIB is the U.S. affiliate of the International Chamber of Commerce). The USCIB is particularly concerned about transborder data flows and the EU Directive on Privacy Policy (see Chapter 5) and is involved in finding a consistent, self-regulatory solution that will allow international business to grow.

With the FTC and governmental regulation in the wings, the United States Council for International Business (USCIB) offers a "privacy diagnostic" designed to help companies ward off government regulation.[4] The USCIB and its Working Group on Privacy

4. http://www.uscib.org/policy/privmin.htm.

and Transborder Data Flows developed the diagnostic that addresses the collection and control of data, how it is used and stored, redress principles, and other questions related to privacy practices. The diagnostic serves as an educational tool to help companies understand the importance of protecting privacy, thereby avoiding government legislation through self-regulation. At this writing, the USCIB does not offer a "wizard" or seal program.

PriceWaterhouseCoopers

PriceWaterhouseCoopers (PWC) offers a full range of privacy consulting services including a review of privacy policy, compliance programs, operational reviews, system security, privacy audits, and recommendations on and installation of privacy tools. These services appeal primarily to larger corporations with a budget that can absorb the higher cost of a "Big Five" consulting company such as PWC.

IBM Security and Privacy Services

Similarly, IBM offers a full suite of workshops, assessments, strategy creation and implementation, all carrying a hefty price tag that appeals to large corporations. For example, the one-day Privacy Workshop costs $5,000. The workshop and a follow-up report on management recommendations and required actions increases the cost to $10,000. Privacy Strategy and Implementation Services range from $50,000 to $250,000 depending upon the services selected.

The Future of Privacy Policies

A review of privacy policies and statements from a number of organizations highlights the general agreement over what should be in a privacy statement but underscores a lack of consensus as to how privacy policies should be implemented. Should e-commerce be trusted to self-regulate by implementing and enforcing its own privacy policies and procedures, or should the FTC step in and impose strict rules and regulations to protect the consumer (something that many privacy advocate groups call for)? However this drama plays out, it is obvious that every company that does business on the Internet, regardless of its size, needs a privacy policy that anyone can locate, read, and understand.

PART 2

Tools to Build Customer Confidence

Platform for Privacy Preferences

One approach to winning and keeping a customer's loyalty is to give him more control over how his personal information is used. Some companies are offering this choice by adopting the Platform for Privacy Preferences, or P3P, in addition to posting privacy policies on their sites. In a nutshell, P3P allows the consumer to automate how his personally identifying information is used, thus obviating the need to read each site's privacy policy.

P3P and the W3C

Work on the platform began in 1997 by the World Wide Web consortium, or W3C, AT&T labs, and corporations such as Microsoft, IBM, Proctor & Gamble, Hewlett-Packard, Engage.com, and American Online, who generally promote self-regulation over government legislation (see Figure 6-1). The latest specification, P3P 1.0, is being promoted by the W3C, and defines the mechanisms for associating privacy policies with Web resources.

The P3P, sometimes referred to as a "social technology" (i.e., not so much a matter of technical implementation as it is the implementation of a set of behaviors), is a protocol that is attempting to standardize the vocabulary of privacy protection, enabling Internet browsers to read automatically privacy policies that appear on participating Web sites. It accomplishes this by embedding technology in the user's browser that automatically confirms whether a site meets the user's predefined privacy preferences.

The P3P 1.0 Specification defines:

• The P3P base data schema, a standard structure for data that a Web site chooses to collect. The P3P base data schema identifies the basic data structures, including four data element sets: user, third party, business, and dynamic. These data structures are populated with values at the time a user or business identifies privacy preferences. Users and/or businesses may provide values for

Figure 6-1   P3P Compliant Web Sites

www.aol.com	www.att.com	www.att.net
www.cdt.org	www.engage.com	www.hp.com
www.ibm.com	www.idcide.com	www.ipc.on.ca
www.pg.com	P3ptestbed-1.w3.org	Vineyard.net
www.w3.org	www.whitehouse.gov	
www.fecht-ag.f2s.com	www.microsoft.com	

Source: http://www.w3.org/P3P/compliant_sites.html.

the user, third party, and business data sets whereas dynamic data sets contain values created during a user session. These data sets contain information read by programs called user agents the purpose of which is to fetch a site's privacy policy and compare it with the user's preferences. User agents can be built into Web browsers (such as Netscape), browser plug-ins, or proxy servers.

As you might expect, user data contain demographic information about the user: name, age, gender, occupation, etc.

Third-party data allow the individual or company to create values for a related third party. An individual might, for example, provide data about a spouse or business partner as the specification suggests. The structure of the third-party data set is identical to that of the user data set.

The business data set is a subset of the user data set tailored to the needs of businesses. (The P3P specification describes these data sets and their use in greater detail in the specification appendices.)

• A standard set of data uses, recipients, categories, and other disclosures. P3P policies encode the P3P vocabulary in XML to identify the types of data collected and how they will be used, who will receive the data that the site collects, and other policy information such as how disputes are resolved and where the user can find the site's text version of its privacy policy.

• An XML format used to express a privacy policy. XML is an attempt to standardize the definition of common data elements across the Internet, and it is in this format that a site's privacy policies are stored.

• A mechanism for connecting user-defined privacy policies with their associated Web pages or Web site. This is the technical means, typically the HTTP protocol (although the consortium is considering other associative protocols in the future), used to relate a site's privacy policies to its Web site.

• A vehicle for moving P3P policies over HTTP. In other words, the P3P policies are accessible by user agents.

How P3P Works

Figure 6-2 illustrates the communication between the user and the Web site, and how their respective privacy is invoked when P3P is in place. At a general level, when a user enters an address in their browser, one of the things the user is doing, unbeknownst to them, is fetching the Web site's privacy polices from the server.

Figure 6-2   Making Your Web Site P3P Compliant

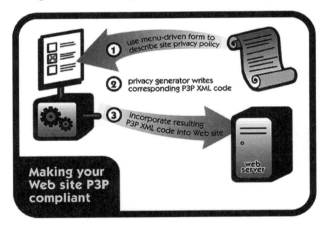

Source: http://www.w3.org/P3P/brochure.html. Copyright © 1997–2000 World Wide Web Consortium, (Massachusetts Institute of Technology, Institut National de Recherche en Informatique et en Automatique, Keio University). All Rights Reserved. Last revised 09/13/2000. http://www.w3.org/Consortium/ Legal/.

The user's preferences are then retrieved and compared with the Web site's policies. If the site's policies are in keeping with the user's preferences, the initial (display) page, typically the home page, is sent to the user's browser. (If the home page is asking for more than, say, data found in standard HTTP access logs and the user's preferences do not allow this, the browser would display a message stating such and allow the user to exit the site.) As the user moves around the site, if the site has more than one privacy policy, for example one for "browsers" and another for "shoppers," the same process will be followed based on what the user does once they enter the site.

Let's look at a hypothetical implementation of a privacy policy using P3P based on an example in the P3P specification. The W3C uses a hypothetical store called CatalogExample.com to demonstrate how a P3P implementation would work.[1] Assume that CatalogExample.com has created and posted its privacy policies on its Web pages, and Judi visits the site using her P3P-enabled browser.

Judi enters CatalogExample.com's address into her browser, which automatically reads the privacy policy for the initial page (remember that a site can have more than one privacy policy based on content and use, something that is explained below). This policy indicates that CatalogExample.com's home page only collects data found in the standard HTTP access logs and nothing else (i.e., the origin of the request: the IP address or Domain Name Service (DNS) name), the time of access, the requested resource, and additional technical information. Judi's browser, which she earlier loaded with her privacy preferences, compares her stored preferences with the site's policy request on the initial Web page.

1. http://www.w3.org/TR/2000/WD-P3P-20000510/.

Assuming that Judi specified that this kind of data collection is acceptable, the site's home page displays on her browser. In this way, P3P will check Judi's preferences before her initial entry into the site so that she never has to reveal any personal information except that which she allows.

Judi has come to this Web site because she is looking for a birthday present for her husband, Steve. She clicks on the link that takes her to the online catalog. This area of the site is more complex. It involves the use of "cookies" that are required for the shopping cart feature on the page, and because this page is gathering more information than the home page (possibly information about her computer and other Web sites she has visited), a separate privacy policy is invoked. Again, let's assume that this practice is in keeping with Judi's preferences, so the catalog is displayed without any popup windows or warnings.

Judi knows what Steve wants (he left her a note about a fly-fishing rod he desperately wants, but Judi and Steve live in a small town with no sporting goods store nearby), so she clicks on the rod (and new flies to boot!) and proceeds to the checkout page. In order to complete the transaction, Judi must provide personally identifying information: her name, address (both physical and e-mail), telephone number, and method of payment. This information is covered by yet another privacy policy because of the sensitive nature of the information being gathered.

Judi's browser checks the privacy policy. She has indicated in her preferences that she wants to be warned prior to giving out her phone number. A pop-up window warns her that her phone number is being requested while explaining how her phone number will be used. Judi could have alternatively specified that she wanted to receive the warning only if her phone number would be sold to a third party (e.g., a marketing research firm for a competing sporting goods store) or used for purposes other than to complete the transaction, in which case she would have received no prompts. However, in this instance, her phone number will only be used to contact her in case there's a problem with delivery, so Judi completes the transaction. Three days later, Steve is surprised with his new fly-fishing rod.

This is just one example of how a privacy policy might be defined and accessed by a customer, illustrating the interaction between the online store and the shopper. The enforcement of the privacy policy is automatic while giving the customer every opportunity to review it when necessary. Next, we need to look at how your company creates its privacy policies.

Creating Privacy Policies for P3P

To the company, P3P is perceived as a series of multiple choice questions about the important aspects of its Web site's privacy policies. (A high-level diagram from the W3C's brochure is seen in Figure 6-2.)

The answers to these questions direct how a Web site browser reacts to user preferences with the Web site, or in the example above, what information Judi is willing to share with the site. Should a company want to adopt the P3P as its privacy platform, the W3C recommends the following steps:

1.   Write a privacy policy for your company. If one is already written, consult with its authors and determine when the policy was written, what the policy is based on, what the author's experience with privacy policies is, and other information pertinent to helping you evaluate its efficacy. Your policy should detail the

data you collect, how you use them, who has access to them, and how long you retain the data. Later, this information will be input into the P3P generator, whose output will be a version understood by the computer.

2. Next, find out how many Web pages you have on your site and decide whether or not you need more than one privacy policy (consider the example above). Different data collection techniques and purposes within the same site could result in policies that are page specific. The P3P allows you to create one general privacy policy for the entire site, but the guidelines also recommend that you consider separate policies that you relate to different pages within your site.

For example, the P3P specification discusses separate policies that our hypothetical company, CatalogExample.com, might use for two different classes of consumers. The first group simply browses the pages but does not purchase anything from the catalog (perhaps a comparison shopper). In this case, CatalogExample.com may collect information about the individual's computer and sites he or she has visited in order to improve their own site, but nothing more. The individual would not be required to provide personally identifying information.

A second group, one that purchases products from the catalog, would be required to provide personally identifying information to complete the transaction: name, address, telephone number, and financial information (e.g., credit card number). The individual could choose to store this information on his computer (via a cookie) to speed up future transactions with the assurance that he could later access and update or correct it, or he could choose not to save the information, instead choosing to reenter the information each time. Thus the "browsers" and "buyers" would have separate privacy policies on the same site. This could potentially make it easier for the company and individual alike to understand and follow a site's privacy policies. Keep in mind that the individual would still be able to access the general privacy policy posted on the site regardless of how it is implemented.

3.   Now take the privacy policy you created in step 1 and select one of the following policy generators to create your privacy policy:

- IBM P3P Policy Editor (http://www.w3. org/P3P/ imp/IBM/)

- PrivacyBot.com (http://www.privacybot.com/)

Figure 6-3 shows the second page of PrivacyBot.com's questionnaire. Note that PrivacyBot.com asks specific questions about what data are collected, how they are used, and whether or not the user may access the information and modify it.

Using the current P3P specification as your guide (readily obtained from http://www.w3.org/TR/P3P/), you will also have to enter the following information into the generator:

- **Entity.** Your identity and how you can be contacted (e.g., The Generic Product Company can be reached at 1–800-Generik or by e-mail at contact@generic. com).

- **Disclosure.** Where on your site your policy is posted (e.g., Our Privacy Policy can be found on our homepage at www.generic.com).

Figure 6-3   PrivacyBot.com's P3P Questionnaire

PrivacyBot.com℠

Home | About | Get Started | Account Manager | Pricing | Eligibility Standards | Terms of Service | Links

Step 2
What Information Do You Collect from Site Visitors?

Please check only the categories of information below that your site collects:

☐ **1. Real-World Contact Information**
name, address, phone, fax or other physical-world contact info

☐ **2. Online Contact Information**
email address, screen name, instant messaging identifier

☐ **3. Government-Issued Identifiers**
social security number, other tax ID or government ID

☐ **4. Non-Financial Identifier**
user ID and password, social security no., or other non-financial ID

☐ **5. Purchase Information**
specific to one transaction, such as payment method

☐ **6. Financial Information**
history of financial accounts, balances, transactions

☐ **7. Information About the User's PC**
user's IP address, processor serial no., browser type or O/S

☐ **8. User Navigation and Clickstream Data**
browsing habits, such as web pages visited and for how long

☐ **9. Data Showing Use of Interactive Features**
active user input, such as search queries or purchases made

☐ **10. Demographic, Social or Economic Data**
gender, marital status, age, income, job or other classification

☐ **11. Personal Preference Data**
favorite color, music, books, cars, hobbies or other interests

☐ **12. Online Postings and User Content**
chat postings, forum discussions or instant messages

☐ **13. Political Information**
membership in political parties, trade unions, churches

☐ **14. Health Information**
physical/mental health history, interests, related purchases

The next step will ask you details about each of the categories you selected.

[Proceed to Step 3]

Reproduced with permission of PrivacyBot.com.

- **Assurances.** What third party or law guarantees that you are following your policy (e.g., Our Privacy Policy is compliant with the Safe Harbor Privacy Principles and is approved by the Better Business Bureau).

- **Data Collection and Purpose.** What data are you collecting, and how are you using it? (e.g., Your phone number and address are requested for shipping purposes only and will not be sold to a third party).

4. The P3P specification currently identifies fourteen specific data categories, as well as an "other" for unspecified categories. Categories are attributes of data elements that make it easer for users and user agents to surmise the purpose of the data elements. Several of the categories include:

- Physical contact information

- Online contact information

- Purchase information

- Financial information

- Computer information

- Navigation and click-stream data

- Demographic and socioeconomic data

- Political information

- Health information

- Preference data

You should categorize your data according to these groupings, and you should specify "other" only after reviewing the categories and verifying that none of them apply. Also, P3P asks you to identify who can access the data. Finally, you must specify retention periods for your data, anywhere from "no retention" to "indefinite retention."

Complete the required fields in the P3P generator (you will be prompted for any missing information), and save the policy using the name policy1.xml. XML is the *lingua franca* of the P3P specification, making user preferences known to privacy policies, and vice versa. If your site requires more than one policy (e.g., one for browsing and one for purchasing), name them consecutively (i.e., policy2.xml, policy3.xml, etc.). Be sure that you enter all data descriptions discussed in step 3 (contact address, disclosure, assurances, and data collection and purpose) in the entity field. P3P provides this information in a "human-readable" format so the user can access and quickly read important information.

5. The policy generator should also create a reference file that instructs a computer's Web browsers where to find your privacy policy on a given page. This file should be saved as policy3p.xml, which you should then upload along with your policy files to your server's root directory

The following example (Figure 6-4) shows the XML, taken from the P3P 1.0 Specification, for a sample policy reference file.

In this example, the file policy1.xml refers to all files excluding those found in the catalog, cgi-bin, and servlet directories. Policy2.xml refers to all files under the catalog directory. Policy3.xml covers the directories cgi-bin and servlet.

6. Finally, you should check your work and make sure you haven't made any mistakes. You can do so by visiting any URL at the site ww3.w3.org/P3P/validator.html and check it for errors. Known as "integrated validation," the user supplies the URL of the target Web page at this site, and the function checks if the Web page is complaint with P3P. You can add your Web site to a list of P3P-enabled sites by going to http://www.w3.org/P3P/compliant_sites.

Figure 6-4   Sample Policy Reference File (XML)

```
<POLICY-REFERENCES
  xmlns="http://www.w3.org/2000/P3Pv1"
  xmlns:web="http://www.w3.org/1999/02/22-rdf-
  syntax-ns#">
<web:RDF>
  <POLICY-REF web:about="/P3P/Policy1.xml">
    <PREFIX>/</PREFIX>
    <EXCLUDE>/catalog/</EXCLUDE>
    <EXCLUDE>/cgi-bin/</EXCLUDE>
    <EXCLUDE>/servlet/</EXCLUDE>
  </POLICY-REF>
  <POLICY-REF web:about="/P3P/Policy2.xml">
    <PREFIX>/catalog/</PREFIX>
  </POLICY-REF>
  <POLICY-REF web:about="/P3P/Policy3.xml">
    <PREFIX>/cgi-bin/</PREFIX>
    <PREFIX>/servlet/</PREFIX>
    </POLICY-REF>
  </web:RDF>
</POLICY-REFERENCES>
```

Source: http://www.w3.org/TR/2000/WD-P3P-20000510/. Copyright © 2000 World Wide Web Consortium, (Massachusetts Institute of Technology, Institut National de Recherche en Informatique et en Automatique, Keio University). All Rights Reserved. http://www.w3.org/Consortium/Legal/.

Figure 6-5 illustrates the transaction flow with P3P once it's implemented in the Web site correctly.

P3P Proponents and Detractors

The biggest hope of proponents of P3P is that it will automate the process of implementing privacy policies and strengthen the case

Figure 6-5   A P3P Transaction Using HTTP

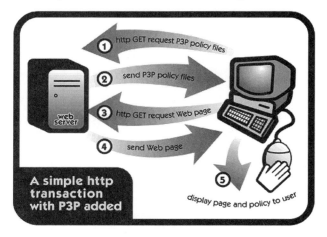

for self-regulation. The P3P platform, once standardized, could potentially save consumers the task of reading privacy policies at participating sites and help protect them from themselves (e.g., by unintentionally providing personally identifying information), hopefully resulting in more online transactions.

However, some privacy advocates are not as enthusiastic about the P3P specification as the W3C. Gary Clayton, CEO of the Privacy Council consulting firm, feels that privacy systems cannot be solely technical. "What will work is a legal structure that sets what our rights are," Clayton stated.[2] The concern from many pri-

2. Scott Tillet, "Spec a First Step for Privacy . . . ," *Internet Week*, July 10, 2000, Issue 820.

vacy groups such as the EPIC and Junkbusters is that companies and the government might think of P3P as a cure-all that would preclude a need for further laws or regulations. They feel that there is no "silver bullet" that will solve the privacy problem. As technology advances, companies and governments should constantly be aware of potential privacy infringement and should update their policies accordingly. The Center for Democracy and Technology (CDT) counters that P3P should be considered a part of the foundation for privacy protection that includes legislation and other privacy tools.[3]

Other concerns are more technical in nature. Some critics feel that P3P, which uses XML to shuttle information between a Web server and a Web browser loaded with an individual's privacy preferences, is too server-centric. In other words, because the only communication is between two computers, there is no way for the individual to know if a site is really complying with its stated policies. The machinations of the server are too far removed from the user and the user cannot readily verify its processes.

Chris Oakes, writing for *Wired* magazine, also sees challenges in understanding human behavior with relation to privacy principles and codifying them into a standard rule set. "The protocol has an odd goal: to arrange communication that is not technical— like two modems handshaking—but human, like two people haggling," Oakes states.[4] In other words, the technical feat of communication will not be difficult, but interpreting the significance of that contact will be difficult. There's no way to predict just how a user will react to the technical exchange or to a company's privacy policy.

3. *Security Wire Digest*, Vol. 2, No. 24, July 3, 2000.
4. Chris Oakes, "The Trouble With P3P," http://www.wired.com/new/topstories/0,1287,13242,00.html.

Critics such as Oakes simply feel that P3P will overwhelm the average site owner, who, nontechnical by nature, will have difficulty understanding the vocabulary involved with setting up P3P. By the time the site owner begins to understand what is involved, he will be too discouraged to pursue it. The need to keep any such technology simple is recognized by all. But can this be done?

The W3C has decided to implement features of P3P gradually while allowing the public to "field test" simpler versions of the protocol. The feeling is that once users grasp the fundamentals of P3P,[5] they will be more willing and able to accept additional and more sophisticated features. And yet this striving for simplicity might result in a watered-down version of P3P that will lead users to question whether the software is really in control. Can the software really be trusted?

Still others such as AT&T's Lorrie Faith Cranor, a researcher in the Web Consortium's P3P Interest Group, feels that prepackaged privacy preferences supplied by trusted vendors such as the Better Business Bureau Online might be another, better alternative. Such organizations would help the user define preferences in keeping with their own philosophy that the user would then simply download to her browser. "My ideal world is I get these prepackaged configurations then go into my browsers and change the nitty-gritty," Cranor said.[6]

In Chapter 9 you'll see more detail in the alternative Seal Programs and the kind of "prepackaged" configurations that Cranor describes.

5. http://www.w3.org/P3P/.
6. http://www.w3.org/P3P/.

P3P Implementation Checklist

Adopting P3P on your e-commerce systems shows strong evidence of your concern for protecting your users from privacy problems. To implement the specification on your site, use the following checklist as a guide for building a customized P3P installation:

• Develop a comprehensive privacy policy that will serve as an input to the P3P Generator.

• Determine the need for additional privacy policies that cover user activities that may require separate or more rigorous controls over data.

• Visit one of the policy generators mentioned in the chapter to translate your human-readable assertions into one a computer can understand and process.

• Categorize your data according to P3P groupings and complete the questionnaire along the fourteen data dimensions.

• Implement the P3P Policy References File and associated files into your Web server configuration (guidance is available at www.w3c.org/p3p).

• Test your configuration and validate that it meets your intent and is consistent with your public privacy policies.

• Share your compliance to P3P with the rest of the world by adding a link to your site at the P3P-compliant site registry.

7

Server-Based Security Countermeasures

Chapter 6 looked at one technology geared to protecting the privacy of e-commerce site shoppers and buyers, but it's of little use if the framework underlying the platform is insecure. Although the topic of security on Internet-attached networks easily fills a book (see *The Complete Guide to Internet Security* by Mark S. Merkow and James Breithaupt, AMACOM Books, 2000), this chapter highlights some of the common countermeasures that organizations use to protect their networks from hostile attacks.

As corporate networks continue to expand and grow well beyond their traditional boundaries, the need to control access to the network increases as well. Some experts believe that more than 50 percent of network attacks occur inside the company from people we know and trust—employees and contractors—attacks that are becoming increasingly difficult to detect, as the edge of the network perimeter grows fuzzier. As the number of new B2C and B2B customers and vendors who connect to your network via the Internet extranets and dial-up access lines grows, the reliance on firewalls alone becomes insufficient.

Dimensions of Logical Access Control

To mitigate some of the problems of attacks from knowledgeable insiders, security countermeasures include a variety of logical access controls that network administrators must heed to make an Internet-attached network more secure. Logical access controls include:

• File access permissions that restrict who can access data and under what conditions (read, write, delete, etc.).

• Execution/escalation privilege that locks down application software to those with permission to use it.

• Access control lists (ACLs) that provide explicit privileges to access a resource (network drives, etc.).

• Host name and IP restrictions that lock down traffic to or from other specific hosts or IP addresses.

• User and password authentication to further restrict access to individuals and provide individual accountability for all activities they perform while they're logged in.

• Strong authentication using Digital Certificates to provide a two-factor mechanism (what someone has combined with what someone knows) that prevents user ID "hijacking."

These controls are typically implemented by a system administrator on the server and consequently are referred to as server-side or host-based security countermeasures.

If you fail to properly secure any of the typical Internet-based services you provide to public users (Web, mail, FTP, etc.), seasoned hackers see the situation as an invitation and opportunity to exploit the servers themselves through known vulnerabilities that you should close down soon after a patch is released.

This problem is particularly prevalent in vendor applications in which the product may not be properly configured "out of the box" for the environment in which it will operate. Secure data transmission protocols or payment systems are frequently included as part of a commercial-off-the-shelf (COTS) or ERP system, but the security of the hosting server itself must be properly configured, maintained, and constantly reevaluated as business needs change and new vulnerabilities to the system are discovered. In other words, software that you purchase cannot be relied upon to protect itself—even the strongest encryption system becomes worthless if the keys it uses are left unprotected.

The task of implementing server-side or host-based logical controls, such as file access permissions or user authentication, requires the active participation of the system administrator, business partners, and other key figures involved with controlling access to critical corporate and customer data. These individuals must understand where and how their servers are vulnerable, institute the appropriate policies to address the problems, and enforce them rigorously.

Web Server Security

The Web server or HTTP network service is an essential component of an electronic commerce infrastructure. Security and business specialists should review all the network services that are being offered on open server ports to decide which are truly necessary to a company's business and mission.

Do you really need to provide network services on all available ports? Chances are, close scrutiny of these services will reveal that many of them are unnecessary and only expose the company to excessive risks for exploits to known vulnerabilities such as buffer-overflow or denial-of-service attacks. The more doors and windows a house has, the more opportunities robbers are given to break in and steal.

However, a house without doors and windows is a bunker—a gloomy and uninviting fortress whose only purpose is security. Security is not an end-all-and-be-all, but one of several aspects of the larger e-commerce model. This model must offer a rich set of services to its users and customers while preventing hostile attacks and intrusions by hackers. A sound security strategy must discourage intruders while reassuring customers.

How is this feat accomplished? As most security experts agree, a far-reaching security policy is the best approach to securing a Web complex. The primary job of your system administrators is to understand and control access to the network and resources through sound security policies, and to help you to guarantee that the network servers are not the weak links in the overall security chain. To do so, administrators must properly harden the complex.

On typical servers, administrators have root access and privileges, and the system administrator (SA) is known as the super user—a role that grants the most privileges. The SA essentially owns the files and directories on the system and controls access privileges to individuals and user groups. To best protect these resources, your security policy should require close examination of file access by the system administrator and determine what access levels are required by users and departments within the company. Furthermore, it's advisable to restrict severely the uses of the "root" or "administrator" accounts by placing unique IDs for your privileged users into the roles of administrator to help in implementing individual accountability. Effective auditing of all privileged user activities is also strongly recommended.

File Access Permissions

Two classes of files on Web servers—the *server root* and *document root* files—contain critical data whose access should be controlled by file-access permissions. The server root directory contains those files that are included and needed as a part of the Web server installation and other critical system files (e.g., configuration, administration, log, and Common Gateway Interface (CGI) program source and executable files). These files should be visible and accessible only to the system administrator and to no one else, internal and external users alike.

The second class of critical server files, the document root, contains the Web pages that are displayed to users as the Web daemon (httpd) patrols the network ports (by default, port 80 and 443 for SSL or https traffic). Usually written in the HyperText Markup language (HTML), these sensitive documents are the most visible aspect of a company's e-commerce site. If a hacker gains access to the HTML files, he can easily modify them and embarrass—or even worse—expose a company to extreme losses.

There is also a third type of file, the log files, which should be secured. They keep track of who accesses the site, the number of requests made, the source IP address of the user, and may be useful to calculate usage or other financial transaction costs. Hackers often cover their footprints before leaving a site by modifying or erasing any trace of their activity in the log files—yet another reason to secure them.

Execution Privileges

Execution privileges define what rights authorized users have to access, modify, create, or delete files on the server. If server processes are given the same access rights as the super user (root), an unauthorized user can wreak havoc on system files by escalating their privileges through exploiting weaknesses in programs that run with root or administrator rights (e.g., buffer-overflow attacks on Web server software, which is analogous to putting ten pounds of potatoes into a five-pound bag—the system simply breaks down).

How can this happen? When the SA installs the Web server, he does so with super-user authority in order to configure the network and listener ports. Network daemons (server processes) can and do invoke subordinate processes, called child processes. These child processes often do everything from serving up Web pages to satisfying requests through invoking CGI scripts or API calls. If the SA is not careful, he can inadvertently grant authority to these lower level processes as well as the daemon that invokes them.

You don't need to strain your imagination too hard to see the potential dangers here. A hacker would have little trouble exploiting a child process or a poorly written CGI script to gain super-user access and control the system files. Once the door is open to the intruder, he can do everything—from stealing passwords, to creating new accounts, pilfering sensitive corporate and customer information, using your system to launch an attack on an outside system, or simply render the server useless.

So what's the solution? SAs should configure all servers to ensure that subordinate processes execute as nonprivileged users, i.e., nobody. This reduces the risk of exploitation by keeping security access at the correct levels—and nothing more!

Automatic Directory Listing

A danger lies in the absence (on some Web server software) of an index file (i.e., index.html). If the Automatic Directory Listing option is turned on when the server boots up and an unwanted user browses the directory, he will automatically obtain a listing of the files in the directory. If this directory happens to contain or point to system files such as CGI scripts, he could gain access to sensitive program source code, examine its contents, find holes if they exist, and return to exploit them later on.

The countermeasure here is to turn off Automatic Directory Listing when you install the server in the first place. Note that this option is turned *on* as the default on most configurations and must be actively reconfigured to *off*.

ACLs

With the proliferation of intranets and extranets comes an increasing concern about company documents and files. Employees now have electronic access to human resource policies and guidelines, corporate strategies, white papers, organizational structures, and a myriad of internal and highly sensitive information on the company intranet.

They make travel arrangements, file travel and other expense reports, change contributions to company 401K plans, and perform other financial transactions. Meanwhile, customer access is restricted to specific files and directories on the Web server—obtaining only those privileges needed to transact their business. The SA's challenge is to grant privileges specific to both the employee and customer while preventing everybody from accessing files and documents that they shouldn't see. Access control mechanisms allow the system administrator to perform this task.

One of the most common techniques for controlling user access on the server is the ACL. ACLs contain names (IDs), passwords, and the types of operations that users are allowed to perform on each resource that's protected. ACLs can also define the hosts (IP addresses) that are permitted to access particular Web pages based on their host names or IP address and, conversely, prohibit those same hosts from accessing specific Web pages. Security experts in the commercial world recommend that it is best to first deny access to everyone and then allow specific users in. The ACL list can work well if properly configured, although this is often a laborious task.

Once secure zones have been determined, authorized IP flows are established. The rule of thumb in the security community is: "All that is not expressly allowed is denied." By partitioning your networks into secure zones, you can protect it from internal attacks and unauthorized access by limiting access to its resources, and can offer more granular protection (i.e., more specific or lower level) mechanisms that lock-down resources to specific users than what is possible through the use of firewalls alone.

In general, the more discrete your security specifications, the greater control you have over system resources. Because firewalls can only protect a single access point, the use of ACLs helps shore up defenses and prevents back door intrusions into the system. ACLs can also complement the use of internal and external firewalls, routers, and intrusion detection systems.

Host Name and IP Address Restrictions

One of the techniques often used by hackers to break into networks is to mimic the IP addresses of trusted machines and exploit the system, particularly on systems that use packet filtering routers. In this case, the firewall makes its decision to allow or not allow access to a system based solely on the IP address in the IP header of the current packet. A basic access-control mechanism would restrict access to services based on the requester's IP address or host name. The server uses this information along with the DNS to determine what level of access the requester is allowed to services, files, and documents.

DNS, a naming service provided to hosts on the Internet, connects IP addresses with machine names to determine the host's availability. If a machine name and IP address do not agree with what is in the DNS table, the SA is wise to block access as part of his security policy for host names and IP addresses.

User and Password Authentication

In its most rudimentary implementation, a user/password scheme associates a user with a password stored in a file on the server. The

UNIX file system uses the /etc/passwd file for storing password data in a form called a hash or transformation. Hashing is a one-way transformation that's easy to do, but hard to undo. Essentially, the value that's entered by the user is scrambled by software and compared with what's stored. If the values match, then access is granted. The risk with a password-based system is that users tend to select passwords that are easily guessed by an experienced hacker who has stolen a copy of the scrambled password file and begins to attack it using brute force or a dictionary attack, trying to convert some known word into the same hashed value that's stored as the password. Once the hacker has unscrambled user passwords, he can gain access to the system using the privileges assigned to the user ID.

In order to protect the password file, you should deploy a shadow password file that splits out the IDs from the passwords into two files—one that's available to check identities and one that contains the associated passwords, but is protected so that a copy of it cannot be stolen, thus thwarting a brute force or dictionary attack. With this protection in place the hacker's ability to crack the password file is removed entirely.

Also, SA must decide whether to store the password files centrally or distribute them on each of the resources they're designed to protect. If they're stored centrally, all server IDs and passwords are defined in a single file (or shadowed file) that is referenced any time access is requested. Centralizing this control has the advantage of administering user IDs and passwords from a single location, requiring the system administrator to go to only one location to make updates to the ID and password files.

CGI Scripts and Active Server Pages

The Web browsers of today are, in a sense, a higher touch-and-feel version of the old 3270 terminal sessions using an online monitor such as IBM's CICS. What has helped take the Web from the monotony of display-only pages to truly interactive sessions is the CGI and application program interfaces (APIs) built into modern Web server software like NSAPI for Netscape Enterprise Servers and ISAPI for Microsoft's Internet Information Server or IIS. These interfaces are protocols that act upon requests from a client computer to a server.

When a user completes a form on a Web page and clicks on the submit button, the browser gathers the information on the form, inserts it in an HTTP message, and *posts* the appropriate HTTP command on the server. The HTTP server (Web server) retrieves the name of the program to run from the data within the posted form, then invokes the program or resource and passes the data to the application server running CGI and other protocols. These requests typically ask to perform some actions on a database (update or retrieve information based on parameters supplied by the user). Where the Web server invokes a program residing on an application server that then maintains data residing on a database server, you can say that the system is based on a three-tier model. The tiers involved are typically called:

- Web tier

- Application tier

- Database tier

CGI and active programming or scripting languages have helped make the Internet a robust e-commerce marketplace. But they have also left holes in the network that seasoned hackers try to exploit due to sloppy programming practices, insufficient separation of processing duties, or plain ignorance of the threats to Web-based systems. Hackers who can successfully compromise a network can manipulate files to their hearts' content, send files to themselves, execute programs, or even launch denial-of-service attacks that overwhelm the network with more demands for service than it can feasibly process. These scripts are simply sitting targets for hackers because they are source code, not compiled code, and for that reason are easier to read, understand, and exploit.

Often, when you hear about malicious defacement of Web pages, chances are a hacker has found vulnerability in the CGI processor. Unfortunately, this problem has been around for years. Abusing CGI scripts is a popular pastime of hackers, partly because faulty CGI implementations are so widespread.

Some of the steps you can take to help secure your systems against rogue uses of the programming and scripting features of Web servers include:

• Avoid running the HTTP daemon (httpd) as a privileged user. Never begin the HTTP service while logged in as *root*, for example on a UNIX-based host. Rather, create and use an innocuous ID—such as *nobody*—with severely restricted privileges on the server when starting the httpd service.

• Delete the sample CGI scripts from the server that were automatically installed in the cgi-bin directory when you loaded the software. Many of the default scripts that often come with the

Web server software, such as phf.cgi, are easy targets for hackers to exploit.

• Store all your CGI scripts in a central directory (called something other than cgi-bin), and restrict the write-and-delete access to this directory only to those people with SA roles.

• Convert your CGI scripts from uncompiled languages like Perl to compiled versions in languages such as C or C++. This will prevent hackers from obtaining your program source code. Alternatively, you could use the APIs supplied with the major Web server software (Netscape and Microsoft) to take advantage of improvements in technology since the Web's infancy.

• Review the shell scripts used in the development of CGI scripts within your software quality assurance (QA) process, looking for file access errors (opening a file for update when only read rights are needed), checking the bounds in input fields to thwart buffer overflow problems, and scanning for other common programming mistakes.

• If you don't have a QA process, you need to adopt a formal process for reviewing code and looking for vulnerabilities.

Software Vulnerabilities

At this point we've looked at directory structures, access control lists, passwords, file permissions, and holes in CGI scripts. Still, with the exception of Java applets that are intended to run in what is called the security sandbox, a method used to prevent damage caused by memory sharing between Java applications, developers often write programs that put a server at risk.

Two common sense policies address the problem of software vulnerability. First, review server-side programs to make sure you followed Internet systems design and development principles that modern-day programming languages espouse (Java, etc.) to reduce the possibility of security breaches (Bruce Eckel's *Thinking In Java*, Prentice-Hall, 2000, is a good place to start). Second, analyze all your programs carefully as part of a QA process to ferret out design flaws or behaviors that could result in security problems.

Test, Test, and Retest

Unfortunately, security is rarely something that developers focus on when designing new software. Security has been traditionally considered project overhead—an afterthought or "nice to have" if time and budget permit. As project lifecycles shorten in the age of Rapid Application Development (RAD) methodologies, developers have even less time to consider the implications of security in what software they build. Developers are simply more focused on what their code should be doing than on what it should not be doing.

The same applies to testing methodologies. The software community all too often tests expected conditions, not unexpected conditions. They attempt to validate that software functions perform as anticipated, while hackers perform their own kinds of tests to show that the unanticipated is also possible. There is no replacement for a sound software development and testing methodology that make security a fixture of the project planning landscape.

An E-Commerce Security Architecture

Figure 7-1 illustrates the basic design for network security. As you can see, the infrastructure relies upon layers of devices that serve specific purposes, and provide multiple barriers of security that protect, detect, and respond to network attacks, often in real time.

The model in Figure 7-1 offers the border protections needed to keep the network secure using a number of mechanisms running on the perimeter of the network. Routers route and filter packets, firewalls limit traffic by services and ports, and Intrusion Detection Systems (IDSs) detect intrusions as they happen.

Figure 7-1   The Basic E-Commerce Network Security Model

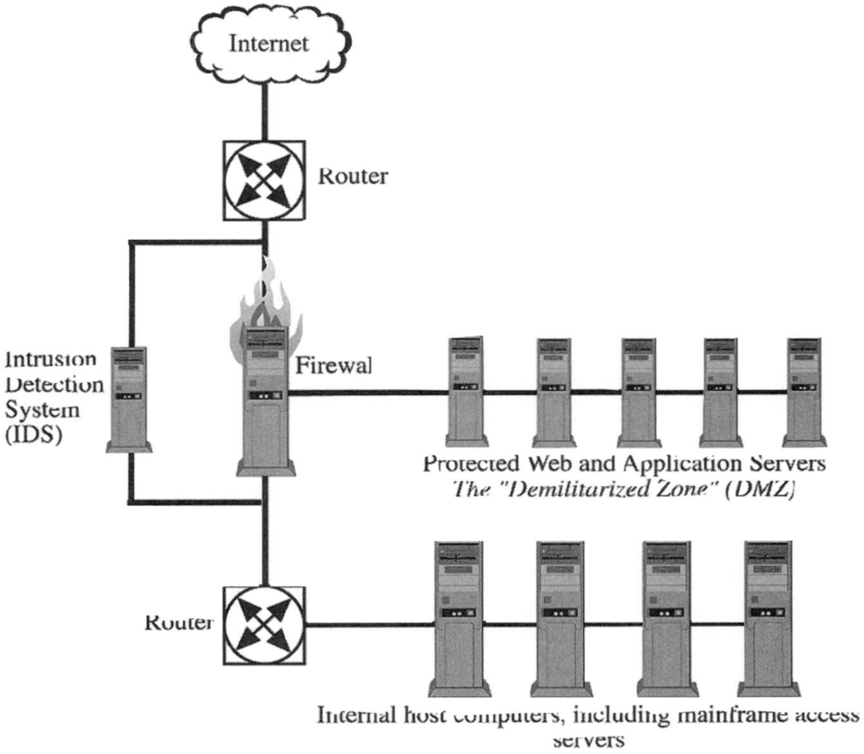

Logical Access Control Through Network Design

It's possible to improve e-commerce network security through more than configuration work and sound program development. One fundamental concept that pervades all secure Internet-accessible installations is the three- or *n*-tier client-server architecture (described earlier).

Security professionals especially embrace three-tier systems for Internet, intranet, and extranet applications. When they're present, these three tiers—Web server(s), application server(s), and database server(s)—greatly reduce many of the threats to production back-office systems and networks, and empower you to perform an excellent job of "border protection."

Three-tier systems benefit everyone in the organization, especially people in IT departments. The model is appealing for enterprise-wide distributed transaction-processing applications because it offers:

• **Centralization** that permits IT to control and secure programs and servers using an already accepted, mainframe-like environment that's scaleable, predictable, and easily monitored. Centralized database services tend to be more optimal because constant monitoring leads to prevention and quick detection of server or network problems.

• Greater **reliability** because equipment resides in a controlled environment that can be easily replicated or moved onto fault-tolerant systems.

• Easier **scalability** because servers or processors can be added to achieve acceptable levels of performance.

• **Flexibility** because well-defined software layers permit the highest degrees of IT responsiveness to changing business needs. With lightweight and inexpensive client desktop requirements, wholesale changes to desktop systems can be made at any time without any effect on the program layer or the database layer, allowing companies to quickly adopt improvements in technology. Additionally, non-PC clients (e.g., POS devices, voice-response units, hand-held devices) can be used at any time because the interfaces to the application are based on open industry standards and are well defined for the developer.

• A **flexible data layer** that enables the reuse of existing mainframe services.

Mainframe services can be made to look just like any other data service layer, thus preserving the transaction processing capabilities of mainframes. This is significant because mainframes tend to be optimal environments for high-volume transaction processing.

These concepts arise from industry-best practices and recommendations from security experts around the world. Because by definition your e-commerce site must be security conscious, you're advised to utilize these principles as much as possible in your own designs. Figure 7-2 illustrates one example of a three-tier network architecture that's not only robust and flexible, but highly secure, too.

Figure 7-2 shows you how it's possible to add security as traffic moves beyond the Web servers into deeper tiers of your network. As traffic moves through the inner firewalls, you can turn off vulnerable services that don't belong there, like FTP, SMTP, HTTP, etc. You can also force the use of trusted hosts to help prevent unwanted requests from processing. You'll see how that's done shortly.

Figure 7-2   Three-Tier "Security Conscious" Architecture

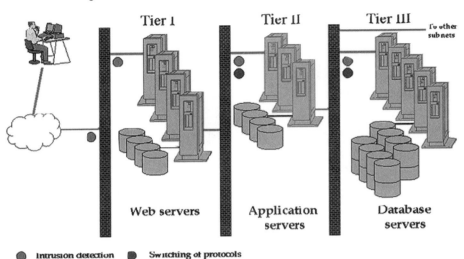

For performance reasons and the lack of any need for specific protection, you might opt to keep your materials "intended for the public" directly within the file systems of the Web servers themselves. Normally, this will only include information that people could otherwise locate via your other advertising channels (catalogs, images, marketing brochures). Any dynamically generated data (stored billing and shipping information, etc.) should be kept as far out of reach of the Internet as possible. Furthermore, any data that your customers supply via Web-based forms should immediately be removed from the Web server through as many firewalls as needed to safely secure it. It's these data that thieves want, so you must be extra careful with their handling. Your customers deserve no less!

This is the most fundamental security precaution that you can take. Never store anything on the Web server itself because you can never really be sure the server will remain constantly in your control. Should a man-in-the-middle attack take place in which a hacker inserts himself in between your legitimate Web server and an unsuspecting visitor to your Web site, perhaps a few Web pages will be spoofed, but your important assets will remain secure.

Another sound measure you can take is to write your application programs to change the protocols it uses as you move into the deeper tiers. For example, your Web forms can invoke a CGI program that then invokes a different program using DCOM or CORBA/IIOP, which in turn calls up a database using ODBC. Because of HTTP protocol vulnerabilities, you don't want your programs running past the outer firewall. Permitting HTTP routing into the back office places you at risk of hackers tunneling through HTTP to try and take over another server. Cut them off at the knees!

With the three-tier approach you can add still more layers of security both between and within each tier. Before the outer firewall, consider using intrusion detection systems to scan for known attack signatures and to automatically alert those in charge of the network—in real time. The uses of cryptography for security both at the transport layer and the application layer are also possible without rewriting programs.

Who Do You Trust?

Trusted hosts are another security measure that you may elect to use. A trusted host limits traffic to a point on the network only from other servers in which a trust relationship has been established. Windows NT enables setting up these trust relationships through network configuration steps, and UNIX-based systems offer tools like TCP wrappers to create trusted host relationships. Using ACLs on your application servers helps to thwart attempts by hackers to run or install programs without the authority to do so. Yet another approach might use server-to-server authentication with digital certificates to provide two-way assurances that application requests and responses are legitimate.

More Controls at the Server

Access control information such as login IDs and passwords is stored on your servers and should be kept in the most obscure forms possible. Never leave this type of information in the clear anywhere on the file systems. Move them to registries on the operating system in encrypted forms or encrypt the configuration files themselves. Even if the server is hijacked, the attacker will still have a hard time accessing other systems or doing anything destructive because they can't access the encrypted access-control information.

On the database tier, consider encrypting the contents—at the field level, the row level, the table level, or the entire database level. Different data classifications call for different situations, so analyze your needs carefully. Where audit trails of activity are crucial (e.g., when customer information is being updated or financial transactions occur), turn on database auditing to help monitor activity or for prosecution purposes.

We've covered switching protocols and closing ports on firewalls, but there's still more to do for improved protection:

• Make certain that your e-commerce servers and any payment system processors are running on separate servers that are insulated from both the Internet and from other domains within your organization. Remove all unnecessary server software that's not specifically for operational purposes. This may include language compilers, Perl libraries, administrative utilities, and factory-supplied log-ins and passwords.

• Firewalls should disallow FTP, telnet, or requests on any open ports.

• Don't operate software such as FTP, telnet, or e-mail systems on any e-commerce server or Web server hardware.

• Whenever remote operations (telnet, xterm, etc.) are needed, make sure the Secured Shell (SSH) and Secure Copy (SCP) are used.

• Make sure httpd and merchant server software (catalog and shopping cart software) is protected against hostile browsers by keeping vendor software patches up to date.

As much as possible, set up your servers to provide unique functions and capitalize on the distributed nature of the network.

Global Secure E-Commerce

In late 2000, Visa International announced two new elements of a Global Secure E-Commerce Initiative designed to increase consumer confidence and merchant profitability on the Internet.

These elements—a Global Data Security Web site for merchants and new operating policies that extend global consumer protections on to the Internet—are part of Visa's ongoing efforts to facilitate universal commerce (u-commerce), defined as the ability to conduct commerce conveniently and securely, any-where, anytime, with any kind of device to extend the traditional e-commerce model of PCs and the Internet.

Global Merchant Data Security Tools

The new Visa global merchant Web site (*www.visa.com/secured*) provides essential tools for merchants in meeting expanded data protection standards for storing and protecting credit card details on merchant sites. The site includes the first comprehensive secu-rity-assessment tool offered for free by a payment organization and allows merchants to understand and adhere to Visa standards surrounding account and transaction information. In addition to the assessment tool, the Web site also features:

• Complete, downloadable guides to Visa's expanded data security standards.

• Visa e-merchant data security best practices.

Here's a quick run down of the Visa's e-merchant data security standards:

• Establish a hiring policy for staff and contractors.

• Restrict access to data on a need-to-know basis.

• Assign each person a unique identity to be validated when accessing data.

• Track access to data, including read access, by each person.

- Install and maintain a network firewall, if data on the network can be accessed via the Internet.

- Encrypt data maintained on databases or files accessible from the Internet.

- Encrypt data sent across networks.

- Protect systems and data from viruses.

- Keep security patches for software up to date.

- Don't use vendor-supplied defaults for system passwords and other security parameters.

- Don't leave papers/diskettes/computers with data unsecured.

- Securely destroy data when no longer needed for business reasons.

- Regularly test security systems and procedures.

- Immediately investigate and report to Visa any suspected loss of account or transaction information.

- Use only service providers that meet these security standards.

Consumer Protection Policies

The new consumer protection policies adopted by the Visa International board in October set global disclosure standards for Web merchants. The new policies require Web retailers to prominently display their privacy policy and online security capabilities.

Visa claims these are practices that have been followed by leading Web merchants for some time and want to mandate these standards to all Visa-accepting merchants globally.

The consumer protection policies also state that in the event of a valid transaction dispute, after the cardholder has made every effort to settle the dispute with the Web merchant but is still not satisfied, the card-issuing bank must provide a refund to the consumer.

Visa's Secure e-Commerce Initiative was launched in July 2000 with the creation of the Payment Authentication Program and the Global Data Security Program. The Payment Authentication Program is based on a new three-domain model called 3DSSL and provides a global approach to authentication—ensuring the parties involved in an Internet transaction are legitimate.

The Visa Secure e-Commerce Initiative is one of several programs Visa launched to promote u-commerce. Other programs include:

• Introduction of an Electronic Commerce Indicator (ECI) that identifies e-commerce transactions on banking records.

• The implementation of a Global Merchant Chargeback Monitoring Program to better track where and why chargebacks occur. Chargebacks are bank-rejected credit card charges to the merchant that typically stem from fraudulent credit card transactions.

• The expansion of mobile commerce (m-commerce) and SmartCard programs to add higher assurances of identity back into electronic and other non-face-to-face transactions.

• Enhancements to Visa's internal processing systems to support increased transaction volumes with enhanced security protections.

Protect Yourself from Yourself

We've taken care of keeping intruders out of the Internet, but now what can we do to protect production systems from internal users attempting access using unauthorized means? More firewalls and IDSs, of course! Add as many internal firewalls with ACLs and IDS sensors to prevent such attacks from your intranet.

You should now be able to see how many of the threats to Internet-attached systems are eliminated, or at least severely reduced, using the approaches above. Are these designs and countermeasures practical? Sure! Is the implementation expensive? You bet! The bigger question, though, is: can you afford to neglect it? You may only have one opportunity to get it right.

"Securing Your Servers" Checklist

Although no single activity is sufficient to secure today's complicated e-commerce systems, the following checklist offers you some "big picture" steps you can take to help reduce everyday computer security problems.

1.   Be careful who you hire to build or maintain your computing systems.

2.   Restrict access to data on a need-to-know basis.

3.   Mandate individual accountability for any activities your employees perform on all production systems.

4.   Periodically check the audit and access logs to ensure that employees aren't accessing data they're not permitted to access.

5. Install and maintain a network firewall both behind your Internet connections and in front of your corporate local area network connections to production systems.

6. Encrypt sensitive data maintained on databases or files and make certain that effective key management practices are used.

7. Encrypt data sent across networks, especially the Internet.

8. Protect systems and data with up-to-date virus protection.

9. Keep security patches for software up to date.

10. Change vendor-supplied defaults for system passwords and other security parameters immediately upon software installation.

11. Securely destroy or dispose of data when no longer needed for business reasons.

12. Regularly test security systems and procedures.

13. Immediately investigate and report any suspected loss of information to the authorities.

14. Make sure that your Internet Service Provider is compliant with industry-best practices for Internet security.

Hands in the Cookie Jar

At the heart of the privacy matter is what some privacy advocates would call the clandestine manner in which Web site sites are, unbeknownst to the user, collecting personally identifying information through stealth technology called "cookies." It's a deceivingly innocuous term for a relatively unsophisticated piece of technology that allows a Web site to collect information about the user and his browsing behaviors on the Internet. Because it's possible that visitors to your Web site will outright refuse any cookies you want to place on their browsers, it's important to understand how cookies work and what you can do to keep your site accessible without them.

Cookies were created by Netscape in 1994 with little fanfare because Netscape envisioned it as a technical solution designed to work in the background to make the user experience on the Web easier. A cookie is a text file with a maximum size of 4k that a Web server places on a user's hard disk. Cookies are embedded in the HTML information that flows between the user's computer and a

Web server. They are usually run from CGI scripts (a method that allows a Web server to send data to and receive data from a database) although they can also be set or read by Javascript. Even if you aren't familiar with HTML (the markup language of Web pages), you should be able to understand the following script that is used to set a cookie:

```
Set-Cookie: NAME=VALUE; expires=DATE;
Path=PATH; domain=DOMAIN_NAME:
Secure
```

Cookies were initially designed to have a life span equal to that of the user session, but many Web servers set the expiration date to a future date that often makes them permanent files on a user's hard drive.

Cookies are based on what the CookieCentral (www.cookiecentral.com) Web site calls a two-stage process. First, they are stored on a user's hard drive when he enters a Web site address in his browser and displays the Web site page (on a Windows system, cookies generally reside in the \\Windows\Cookies directory although this directory structure can vary depending upon machine configuration). For example, when a user decides to go to Lycos.com to sign up for a new account a cookie is created on the user's hard drive. In order to create the account, the user must supply his name, birth date, mailing and email addresses. At this point, Lycos has transferred a text file to the user's hard drive and inserts a unique identification number that identifies the user's browser, but not the individual.

Cookies can have different life spans and vary in the information they store, but in general a cookie contains a unique identifier, the domain name of the site that created the cookie, and any number of variables and values that are site specific, and they can have an indefinite lifespan. Figure 8-1 shows the extract of the cookie file that was created on the author's hard drive. To a human being the text is mostly unintelligible. However, to the Web servers that placed them in the file, the cookie stores a wealth of personal information including the site preferences, browsing habits, and more.

Although many of the Web sites listed in the file extract are members of the TRUSTe seal program (see Chapter 9 for more on seal programs) and have links to privacy policies, it is this kind of unannounced storage of personal information in a cookie on the user's hard drive that has alarmed the public.

The second stage of the cookie process involves the clandestine transfer of the cookie from the user's computer to the Web server. In our example file, users do not need to re-enter previously stored passwords or other personal details when he returns to a Web site that previously placed a cookie entry, because these Web servers already recognize the user's browser identifier and can retrieve personal information saved from previous sessions.

Figure 8-1   Sample Extract of Netscape Cookies File

If Cookies Aren't for Eating,
What Are They For?

As mentioned earlier, cookies were initially envisioned by Netscape as a means of storing user passwords and user preferences. However, the explosion in the number of Internet sites and the rapid growth of electronic commerce have created pressures on Internet companies to differentiate themselves by providing services and creating a "user experience" that no other site has. In the days of yore, gas stations would wage price wars and offer services such as free oil and tire pressure checks, even glassware giveaways, as a way of luring the passing motorist into their station. However, their competition was local and limited to a precise geographic locale. The global reach of the Internet has made the competition so fierce that Web sites struggle simply to keep the loyalty of their customers. They have no friendly attendants greeting you at the pump, checking your tires, or washing your windshield. There is only the computer, the user, and, in between, the user experience.

Because cookies are a key tool for customizing the customer experience on your Web site, the unanticipated expansion in the use of cookies is not surprising, and the consequent public outcry was therefore inevitable. The most prevalent uses of cookies are described below:

• **Site Personalization.** As mentioned previously, because cookies can save the user from having to re-enter his ID and password, they can also remember his preferences. Does he prefer not to see sports news and go directly to the business page where he can get the latest stock quotes on Yahoo? Does he want to see what the latest releases in classical music are on Amazon.com without having to make the same request each time he returns to the site? This kind of personalization is the best face that the Internet can put on an impersonal medium, and is probably the most prevalently used method by Web sites to distinguish themselves from "the guy down the street."

- **"Shopping Cart" Systems.** The shopping cart system used today on many online ordering systems is the equivalent of the brick-and-mortar layaway plan. It allows users to browse the store, make selections, and return later to complete the purchase, with the added convenience that the user never has to leave home. In order for a Web site to "remember" a user's purchases from one session to another, the cookie became a convenient mechanism for storing selections from the online catalog. This activity inevitably led to customer "profiling" whereby a site could make future recommendations to a customer based on his past purchases. This use of cookies is particularly popular at the sites of booksellers and music vendors where products by the same or "like" writers or musicians are suggested to the customer.

- **Tracking Web Site Behaviors.** Many sites now follow the user's footprints as he traverses their Web site. Again, the pressure to constantly improve a Web site has led site administrators to track how customers used the Web site in order to improve their design. They can, for example, determine how many individuals have accessed a specific page, just as they can determine that another page is rarely visited. Some customers object to this kind of surveillance (in a recent class action suit in Texas, plaintiffs have accused Yahoo! of what they call "stalking"[1]).

1. http://www.nytimes.com/library/tech/00/02/cyber/cyberlwa/181aw.html.

• **Targeted Marketing.** If a user were to look in his cookies directory, he would probably notice files whose domain names belonged to sites he had never visited. These files were created by companies that resell ad space belonging to a number of frequently visited sites, much like billboard salesmen. The difference is, companies that put their ads on billboards have a difficult time knowing exactly how many people see their ad and what effect it has on them. So targeted marketing companies, as they are called, such as DoubleClick, Inc. and Interse Corporation, buy ad space on popular Web sites like Yahoo.com then resell the space to other companies who pay to rent the spot. Targeted marketers then, through agreements with advertisers, place third-party cookies on the user's computer as visitors browse the advertiser's site and collect information about their behaviors (like click-throughs and other clickstream data), often without the user's knowledge. Targeted marketers then resell this information to a third party who collates it along with other previously collected user information to dynamically create a customer profile. This is the use of cookies that most enrages privacy advocates and consumers alike (once they learn the truth!).

Advocates of cookies, however, argue that the consumer grows less concerned about cookies once he personalizes his browsing experiences using cookies to save him time and reduce his aggravation of wading through unwanted advertising. Cookie advocates believe that cookies will help to deliver exactly what the individual wants and nothing more. However, according to the Pew survey, only 27 percent of the respondents felt that tracking their behaviors through the use of cookies was helpful.

Cookie Myths

Some persistent stories continue to circulate about the havoc that cookies can wreak such as deleting files from a user's hard drive. This simply isn't true. The controversy surrounding cookies isn't about the harm they can do to a computer but has to do with the way in which they store and pass information about the individual. Out of fairness to the cookie, the following list of concerns highlights myths that need to be debunked:

• **Cookies can access my hard drive.** This is simply not true. Cookies are text files, not executables. They play a passive role in storing data and are not able to scan hard drives, read directories, delete files, or perform any role other than holding information. For this reason they are not capable of spreading computer viruses, another myth about cookies.

• **Cookies from one Web site can be accessed by another site.** False. A cookie can be accessed only by the domain that placed it there.

• **Cookies can retrieve e-mail addresses.** Not true. The only way this can happen is if the user enters his e-mail address on a form and the address is saved in the cookie.

• **Cookies are the only means of tracking a Web site user.** False again. Cookies can be the most persistent form of data tag that identifies the individual, but they are by no means the only way in which a user sacrifices information about himself. Whenever he accesses a Web site, he is revealing his ISP, the operating system and browser, his IP address, and other information about the hardware and software he is using. Although this kind of information may not be as threatening as more personally identifying information, the user should be mindful that by virtue of accessing the Web site, he automatically begins to "leak" data.

Figure 8-2 shows what information you reveal just by visiting a URL on the Internet. The "I Can See You" program from anonymizer.com is one frightening example of what people can collect from a simple visit by your browser. See for yourself at: *www.anonymizer.com/snoop.cgi*

How the Cookie Crumbles?

Given the public outcry over the use of cookies, browser producers such as Netscape and Microsoft are giving users more of a voice in how cookies are used on their computers. Depending upon the browser and the version of the browser that a particular user has installed, he is able to tell his browser that he does not want to accept cookies. Earlier versions of browsers require the user to reject cookies each time a Web site attempts to write to his hard drive (typically browsers numbered below 4.0), but later versions allow the user to set his options to reject cookies once. We're including the basic commands that the user can use to disable (or reactivate) cookies, because you may want to disable them on your own computers for your personal privacy. You can build customer confidence by being conscious of the user's concerns, giving proper notice of cookies, and allowing the customer to opt out. In addition, because your users are able to disable cookies, it's important that your site is still useful if a visitor rejects a cookie

Figure 8-2 "I Can See You" Output Web Page

Privacy Analysis of Your Internet Connection

from

(Please wait for analysis to complete, it may take 2 or 3 minutes)

Related pages: How this analysis works

Network-Tools.com - Run a trace on any computer on the Internet.

The system attempted to place the following persistent cookies on your system. Reload to see if the cookies were accepted

Privacy.net = Privacy Analysis
No Cookie from this site is on your system from prior visits.

You linked from here (if you linked from another web page):

http://www.anonymizer.com/snoop.cgi

Your Browser Type and Operating System:

Mozilla/4.7 (Macintosh; U; PPC)

All information sent by your web browser when requesting this web page:

Accept: image/gif, image/x-xbitmap, image/jpeg, image/pjpeg, image/png, */* Connection: Keep-Alive Host: privacy.net Referer: http://www.anonymizer.com/snoop.cgi User-Agent: Mozilla/4.7 (Macintosh; U; PPC) Accept-Encoding: gzip Accept-Charset: iso-8859-1,*,utf-8

Is JavaScript, VBScript, or JAVA enabled? Text will appear if these features are enabled. The JAVA window may not appear until the page finishes loading.

JavaScript is enabled and working.

Cookie via JavaScript: Privacy.net_JavaScript = ; Priv

The following plug-ins are installed on your system:

Headspace Beatnik Helper Stub Plugin V1.0.1 - Beatnik Helper for Netscape Communicator - Beatnik Stub Plug-In
Default Plug-in - Netscape Navigator Default Plug-in - Default Plug-in
IPIX Plugin PPC V5.304 - - IPIX Plugin PPC V5.304
LiveAudio - - LiveAudio

MRJ Java Plugin - Runs Java applets using an   tag. For more information, please visit the MRJ Plugin web site. - MRJ Plugin
PDFViewer - - PDFViewer
QuickTime Plug-in 2.0 - The QuickTime Plug-in allows you to view a wide variety of multimedia content in web pages. For more information, visit the QuickTime web site. - QuickTime Plugin
RealPlayer(tm) G2 LiveConnect-Enabled Plug-in (Mac) - RealPlayer(tm) LiveConnect-Enabled Plug-in - RealPlayerG2 Plugin
Shockwave Flash - Shockwave Flash 4.0 r20 - Shockwave Flash NP-PPC
Screen Width: 1024
Screen Height: 768
Screen Available Width: 1024
Screen Available Height: 748
Screen Color Depth: 16

You have visited this many web pages this session in this window: 2
The date/time on your computer and time zone is: Mon May 28 13:47:30 GMT-0700 2001
Time/date in your locale format: May 28 13:47:30 2001

Reprinted with permission of Anonymizer, Inc. (http://www.anonymizer.com).

you're trying to place. If you turn away a user because they refuse your cookies, you'll turn away their purchase as well!

For Netscape 3.0 users:

- Select the *Options* menu.

- Select *Network Preferences*, then *Protocols*.

- Under the *Show an alert before accepting a cookie* check the option button.

For Netscape Communicator 4.0 users:

- Click *Edit* on the task bar.

- Select *Preferences*.

- Click on *Advanced*.

- Select your options to accept all, accept selected, or accept none in the box labeled "*Cookies.*"

For Microsoft Internet Explorer 3.0 users:

- Select *View.*

- Select *Options.*

- Select *Advanced.*

- Check the box: *Warn before accepting cookies.*

- The security alert shown in Figure 8-3 then appears.

Figure 8-3   Microsoft Cookies Security Alert

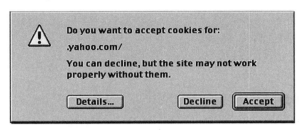

For Microsoft Internet Explorer 4.0 users:

- Select *View.*

- Select *Internet Options.*

- Click the *Advanced* tab.

- Scroll down to the yellow exclamation icon under *Security.*

- Select one of the three options there to regulate your use of cookies.

For Internet Explorer 5.0 users:

- Select *Tools.*

- Select *Internet Options.*

- Click the *Security* tab.

- Click *Internet.*

- Select *Custom Level.*

- Scroll down to *Cookies* and choose one of the two options.

Privacy advocacy sites such as Junkbusters.com encourage users to disable cookies unless they absolutely need to use them. They also recommend using their Internet Junkbuster program, which sits between the user's browser and the Internet. This service checks outgoing HTTP requests for each resource (including graphics) against a list of URLs of advertisers that the user has pre-selected not to see from the Junkbusters.com Web site. If the Junkbuster program determines that the user does not want to see specific advertising, it will block transmission of the content to the user's browser.[2]

In addition to the Internet Junkbuster, a number of other "anti-cookie" tools are available to the user. Cookie Central, for example, offers a number of tools at their site (*www.cookiecentral.com*) that assist users in heeding their recommendation against generally accepting cookies, including:

• **Cookie Web Kit.** Using a simple batch file (.bat), this kit automatically deletes cookie files whenever the user boots up his computer.

• **Cookie Pal.** A management system that allows the user to automatically accept or reject cookies from selected sites.

• **ZDnet Cookie Master 2.** Monitors cookie activity on the user's computer, giving the user access to his cookies, including the ability to delete cookie files.

• **Cookie Crusher 1.5** *The Limit Software.* Automates the rejection of cookies in Netscape Navigator or Microsoft Internet Explorer by eliminating the need to respond to each cookie alert.

2. http://www.junkbusters.com/ht/en/ijb.html.

• **Luckman's Anonymous Cookie for Internet Privacy**™. A free utility that enables the user to disable all cookies in his cookie directory or file.

• **Buzof.** Eliminates cookie warnings by allowing users to close automatically unwanted dialog or message boxes.

The IDcide Privacy Companion

One innovative approach to cookie management comes from IDcide (www.idcide.com). Called the Privacy Companion, it is the first-of-its-kind tool that alerts users when they're being tracked, and by whom.

Most programs designed to bust cookies, including those listed above, can't offer the level of control needed to help people make real-time decisions about how much personal information they're willing to release. Privacy Companion allows the user to decide when to allow tracking by opting in or out with a mouse click. The user then doesn't have to reject cookies from every site he visits or change his browser settings.

"The benefits of our product are unquestionably clear. Most people don't realize that every time they surf the Web they are under surveillance. Internet sites collect every piece of information they can about a Web surfer. The Privacy Companion makes it possible to control how much information web surfers want to give out," claims Ron Perry, cofounder of IDcide.

The Privacy Companion is a freely downloadable add-in for Microsoft Internet Explorer versions 4 and 5, operating on Windows 95/98, NT 4, and Windows 2000. There are no plans to charge for downloading the Privacy Companion.

The tool is most effective in warding off the unwanted cookies that are planted on computers by third-party tracking networks such as DoubleClick (described earlier). When you are visiting a site that is a member of a tracking network, a cookie is placed on your computer that gathers information about your activity on the Internet. DoubleClick is cited as the most common example of a tracking network where Privacy Companion helps out. When you're visiting a site that's attached to a third-party tracker like DoubleClick and Privacy Protection mode is enabled, the Privacy Companion will block unwanted cookies and warn you that you're being tracked. It also provides you information on the sites that have tried to follow you.

Because cookies are the most common means of tracking Web usage, the Privacy Companion works to detect them and automatically blocks their storage on your computer. By focusing on persistent cookies (those that are stored on your hard drive) you will be able to receive personalized services on the sites that deposit cookies directly without the concern or fear that other sites are monitoring your activities or flooding you with banner advertisements. Nonpersistent cookies only exist as long as a browsing session is active.

Browser cookies are a perpetual source of argument as advertisers claim they're a harmless way to make your Web browsing experience better, claiming that you'll only see targeted ads for products that are of interest to customers. By storing pertinent data about a user's preferences in a cookie, proponents argue that cookies personalize the user's experience on the Internet.

Privacy advocates, on the other hand, describe cookies as secretive little spies that hide out on your computer, making Big Brother aware of your every move. While the truth lies somewhere in the middle, there is still plenty to fear if you value your personal privacy.

While most cookie-blocking programs on the Web use an "all or none" approach to blocking cookies, the Privacy Companion offers three privacy "modes" that are changeable as you surf from site to site. Through the interface shown in Figure 8-4 below, you can see when a tracking site is active and what it's trying to track. The three privacy modes are:

- No privacy lets everyone track you.

- Medium privacy blocks third-party tracking network cookies.

- High privacy blocks all cookies.

This separation of privacy settings places the Privacy Companion into a class by itself to meet user demands for control over who's watching who on the Internet.

Figure 8-4   The Privacy Companion Tool Interface

Reproduced with permission of IDCide.

The Final Word on Cookies?

Few organizations, including the staunchest privacy advocacy groups, would argue that cookies should be outlawed categorically. They can, when used prudently and with notification, improve the user's experience on the Internet by eliminating repetitive tasks and introducing him to products and services tailored to his needs and interests. However, the user must also be able to choose when and how cookies are used. Advocates of the "opt in" policy feel that cookies should not be allowed at all unless the user requests them. "Opt out" advocates feel that the user needs to be educated on the role cookies play on the Internet, and he should be given the tools to disable cookies, the tools that are being built in to recent versions of the most popular browsers. Either way, education appears to be key to the continued success of electronic commerce on the Internet. Otherwise, feelings of powerlessness and intrusion into their personal lives will deter potential users as well as experienced users of the Internet from "surfing the Web."

To keep the till running even when users refuse your cookies, you'll want to adopt alternative means to identify a repeat visitor to accommodate their preferences. One good means of accomplishing this without cookies is a log-in page that's useful for authenticating a user and retrieving their preferences. This is the idea behind My Yahoo! and other highly customized sites.

Countering Cookie Crumblers

In Chapter 8 you saw a number of built-in and third-party means to disable cookies on Web browser software, but you don't want the refusal of cookies to prevent users from successfully navigating your site. By understanding there are people out there who remain very concerned about how cookies are used—and abused— on the Internet today, you can still offer the richness and dynamic experiences of browsing by accommodating their needs. Here are a few tips that will help you to keep visitors on your site.

• Check your visitors' browser settings on your home page when they arrive at your site.

• If cookies are disabled, redirect those visitors to Web pages that offer the same features as the cookie-enabled Web pages.

• Give those visitors an opportunity to opt-in to customizing their surfing experiences by providing them a form to create a unique ID and password that is not stored using cookies.

• Provide a preferences Web form for them to select choices appropriate for your system.

• Keep the browsing experience simple for them without extra clicking on links or waiting periods.

Third-Party Seals of Privacy Assurance

With visible seals that attest to your Web site's security and privacy practices, your site visitors, buyers, and B2B partners can better trust that their personal and transactional information will be kept private, secure, and confidential. In this chapter you'll learn what a Web seal program is, where you can find information on seal programs, and how you can participate in these programs.

What Is a Seal Program?

An online seal program is a certification program that allows Web sites to validate their privacy policies while allowing consumers to easily identify Web sites adhering to specified information-practice principles. The consumer typically sees the seal prominently displayed on the home page. Seal programs represent another effort in the move for the online industry to self-regulate. Unlike P3P, however, seal programs require sites to submit to a rigorous application process and perform periodic site reviews after the seal is granted.

Why Is Independent Certification Needed?

Because business owners often assume too much about their internal practices, independent verification of your actual business activities helps you to gain the insights of professionals and would-be data thieves to discover what you'd likely miss on your own. Proponents of seal programs believe the use of third parties—whose goals are to obtain and evaluate business goals and policies—reassures the consumer of the objectivity and reliability of the seal. They also believe that a seal program offers a consistent and predictable implementation of its policies, and that the same principles are applied to small online retailers as to major corporations.

Just as the Underwriter's Laboratories (UL) seal on electrical products and a myriad of other products and systems helps consumers to gain confidence in the manufacturers' claims of safety, Web privacy seals of assurance help your shoppers to gain confidence that the data they share with you will remain safe.

Parts of a Seal Program

A seal program generally has the following components:

• **Seal of Approval.** The token visible on a participating site's display page that indicates the site's participation in the vendor's seal program. This seal indicates that the site has met the required privacy guidelines, including disclosure of the privacy policy, choice (i.e., opt in/opt out), and security.

• **Dispute Settlement.** A seal program should have a formal procedure for resolving complaints or disputes. For example, the consumer should know the exact steps to follow when he feels a Web site has violated its privacy policy. This procedure should be obvious and easy to understand.

• **Ongoing Site Monitoring.** Probably the most distinguishing feature of a seal program, third-party monitoring of a site's policies and adherence to them, ensures a periodic (at least annual) review of privacy practices. With some seal programs, self-assessment is an option although you should ask what additional work this entails, as well as what value you place on having a third-party monitor your site.

• **Enforcement.** A seal program must have teeth. If a Web site violates the guidelines of the seal program and doesn't correct the violation, it could lose its seal and be referred to external agencies including the Better Business Bureau.

Characteristics of a Seal Program

According to the OPA, a seal program should exhibit the following characteristics:

• **Ubiquity.** the seal program should be far-reaching and readily recognizable by consumers (much like the Good Housekeeping Seal of Approval or AAA). This will increase consumer confidence in the brand name.

• **Comprehensiveness.** A seal program should cover data of varying degrees of sensitivity. Personally identifying information such as name, address, telephone number, and social security number would, for example, require more stringent protection measures and guidelines than information such as the pages on a Web site that a customer visited.

• **Accessibility.** The user should easily be able to locate and understand a seal.

• **Affordability.** The cost of the program should not be prohibitive for small businesses, and businesses with simple sites should not be required to pay the same fees as companies with complex sites. Instead, fees should be calculated as a function of the complexity of the site, the amount of data collected, how it is used and distributed, and so forth.

• **Integrity.** A seal provider should be able to enforce its policies and protect the integrity of the seal.

• **Depth.** A seal provider should be able to support its customer base by providing services that back up the seal. For example, a seal should have clearly defined policies and procedures for handling and resolving user complaints about violations of online privacy policies.

How Seals Are Obtained

A number of companies offer seal programs, including:

• Better Business Bureau Online Privacy Program (www.bbonline.org)

- CPAWebTrust (www.cpaWebTrust.org)

- PriceWaterhouseCoopers (www.pwcbetterWeb.com)

- PrivacyBot.com (www.privacybot.com)

- Secure Assure (www.secureassure.com)

- TRUSTe (www.truste.org)

So how do you decide which seal program to use? Most companies are concerned about cost, but you shouldn't let this be your overriding concern. Seal programs typically use a tiered cost structure based on either the complexity of the site and the amount of data collected and how it is used, or the revenue size of the company. BBBOnline, for example, ties its cost structure to the annual sales (offline and online) of the company. A company with $1 million or less in total company sales would pay a one-time application fee of $75 and an annual assessment evaluation fee of $150 (ranging to $5,000 per year for companies with over $2 billion in annual sales).

An advantage of seal programs is the different focuses they have. You can pick one that is most appropriate for your industry or type of business. Although they all generally require the same information and enforce the same principles, seal programs may have differences in alliances or allegiances.

PriceWaterhouseCoopers, for example, has name recognition and a large staff of consultants to back it up. BBBOnline, on the other hand, is backed by the longstanding reputation and ubiquity of the Better Business Bureau and its policies. Keep in mind that part of the objective of a seal program is to reassure the consumer, and certainly programs with household names can't hurt. Privacy protection, however, is not just about psychology; it must be backed by stringent procedures and enforcement. The best advice when choosing a seal program (if this is one of the tools you choose) is to compare philosophies, requirements, cost, and also the client list to see which programs the major corporations are choosing.

Once you have chosen a seal program, you will most likely follow these steps to obtain your seal:

1.   Complete the business application and, in some cases, pay a nominal application fee.

2.   Complete a compliance assessment questionnaire. Such a questionnaire will determine your eligibility for a privacy program seal. You must be able to demonstrate that you have implemented a privacy policy and the appropriate data security measures, and that your information management practices abide by the seal program's policy.

3.   Submit the completed participation agreement to the seal program.

4.   Once your questionnaire has been evaluated and your site has been reviewed for compliance, you will receive instructions on how to install the seal on your Web site.

BBBOnline Privacy Seal

The BBBOnline Privacy Seal signifies that an online merchant meets the highest standards for the treatment of personally identifiable information. Companies that qualify must post privacy notices telling consumers what personal information is being collected and how it will be used. Qualifying Web sites commit to abide by their posted privacy policies, and agree to a comprehensive independent verification by BBBOnline. The privacy program also gives consumers a mechanism for resolving disputes. The BBBOnline's privacy seal is backed by the Council of Better Business Bureaus (CBBB). As an extension of the BBB brand, the BBBOnline's privacy seal carries high name recognition and trust that helps to build consumer confidence.

In April 1997, the Council of Better Business Bureaus recognized the need to gain expertise in Internet commerce and created the BBBOnline subsidiary to specialize in e-commerce consumer protection and business self-regulation needs. To create its privacy program, BBBOnline worked closely with business leaders and representatives from major corporations with expertise and leadership in the e-commerce arena including:

- America Online
- American Express
- AMR Corporation (American Airlines & Travelocity)
- AT&T
- BankAmerica
- Dell
- Dun & Bradstreet
- Eastman Kodak
- Equifax
- Experian
- Ford

- Hewlett-Packard

- IBM

- Intel

- J.C. Penney

- MCI WorldCom

- Microsoft

- New York Times Electronic Media

- Procter & Gamble

- Reed Elsevier (parent company of LEXIS-NEXIS)

- Sony

- US West

- Viacom

- Xerox

BBBOnline will help to resolve customer complaints using the same approach as the offline BBB process. The first step encourages the business and the consumer to resolve the complaint between themselves. If that fails, BBBOnline steps in, providing a consumer-oriented process to resolve the complaint. Businesses that repeatedly violate their own policies will have their BBBOnline seal revoked. They'll then be publicly identified, and the most serious or frequent offenders will have the violations reported to the proper government agency, including the FTC (whose overall mission is antitrust and consumer protection).

The BBBOnline Kids Privacy Program

The BBBOnline Kids Privacy Program is a part of BBBOnline intended for businesses with Web sites directed at children to demonstrate their commitment to protecting children's privacy online. When you see a BBBOnline Kid's Privacy seal, it means that the business has not only met BBBOnline's Privacy seal requirements, but that it is in full compliance with the guidelines of the Children's Advertising Review Unit (CARU) of the Council of Better Business Bureaus.

Web sites that carry the BBBOnline Kid's Privacy seal must:

• Obtain parental consent before any personal information can be collected, used, or disclosed.

• Obtain parental consent before children are allowed to post or communicate directly with others.

• Provide warnings and explanations in easy-to-understand language.

• Avoid collecting more information than necessary to provide children's games and activities.

• Be selective in the other sites to which they link.

• Follow strict rules when sending e-mail.

The BBBOnline Kid's Privacy requirements are based on the guidelines of the OPA, the Council of Better Business Bureaus' Children's Advertising Review Unit, and the Children's Online Privacy Protection Act (COPPA). The BBBOnline seals are shown in Figure 9-1. For additional information about the BBBOnline seal programs, visit the BBB Web site at www.bbbonline.org.

Figure 9-1 The Better Business Bureau's Online Seal Programs

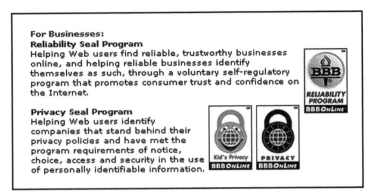

Reproduced with permission of BBBOnLine.

CPA WebTrust

Another initiative comes from the American Institute of Certified Public Accountants (AICPA) and the Canadian Institute of Chartered Accounts (CICA). The CPA WebTrust seal of integrity offers consumers an independent professional's opinion that attests to a merchant's online trustworthiness

WebTrust identifies and helps reduce E-Commerce business risks and encourages online confidence and activity. Through the WebTrust program, you can:

• Identify risks, including possible privacy breaches, security gaps, and other systems affecting the customer interface

• Benchmark and take advantage of best practices in information handling

• Gain independent verification that the site complies with the international WebTrust Standards for E-Commerce.

CPAs, Chartered Accountants, and their equivalents world wide are recognized as trusted, independent third parties who can assure the accuracy and fairness of financial and non-financial information. Only licensed public accountants who complete special training are able to issue a WebTrust seal. Unlike other seal programs, WebTrust requires accountants to conduct an independent examination that carries the professional equivalency of a financial statement audit.

WebTrust relies upon unique standards that apply to business-to-business and business-to-consumer sites and are completing standards for Service Providers. It also has a set of standards that apply to Certification Authorities.

The WebTrust seal (shown in Figure 9-2) is only awarded to your site if it completely passes the examination by a licensed CPA, Chartered Accountant, or equivalent. Clicking on the seal allows your customers to link to the independent accountant's examination report, as well as your site's business practices and privacy policies, the WebTrust Principles and Criteria, and other sites with WebTrust seals.

The WebTrust On-Line Privacy program's advantages include:

• Differentiates your company as leaders in this volatile and increasingly public arena.

Figure 9-2   The WebTrust Seal of Assurance

Reproduced with permission of WebTrust.

• The first and most comprehensive standards for conducting online commerce, including protecting personally identifiable information.

• Encompasses all key facets of online privacy.

• Only program offering certification by CPAs and their equivalents.

• Complies with significant US and international privacy guidelines, regulations, and recommendations.

WebTrust sets an international standard for E-Commerce protection. Developed jointly by the American Institute of Certified Public Accountants (AICPA) and the Canadian Institute of Chartered Accountants (CICA), WebTrust is currently being offered by public accounting professionals in the US, Canada, Australia, England, France, Germany, Hong Kong, Puerto Rico, Scotland, Spain, and Wales.

Your online business receives an on-site review process by the CPA to renew your WebTrust seal at least once every six (6) months. The CPA or equivalent will work closely with you as your E-Commerce consultant to help your site remain in compliance with the WebTrust Principles and Criteria. WebTrust also has a built-in consumer complaint resolution mechanism in relationship with the National Arbitration Forum to use binding arbitration to resolve customer complaints related to privacy violations as well as product or service quality issues.

WebTrust standards have been developed by experts in auditing, accounting, and risk management. These standards also incorporate, whenever possible, prevailing international "best practices" and guidelines for conducting business over the Internet.

In Web We Trust . . .

To further encourage privacy self-regulation, the TRUSTe Program is intended to help companies implement appropriate privacy practices without undue government legislation or specific mandates. The TRUSTe logo (shown in Figure 9-3) symbolizes that a site owner has committed to disclosing the site's privacy practices to the public and is backed by TRUSTe's assurance process. TRUSTe's goals are to provide:

• Online consumers with control over their personal information;

• Web publishers with a standardized, cost-effective solution for both satisfying the business model of their site and addressing consumers' anxiety over sharing personal information online;

• Government regulators with demonstrable evidence that the industry can successfully self-regulate.

Web site owners who participate in the TRUSTe Seal program agree to:

• Disclose their information management practices in their privacy statement.

Figure 9-3   The TRUSTe Seal

Reproduced with permission of TRUSTe (http://www.truste.org).

- Display the TRUSTe mark.

- Adhere to their own privacy practices.

- Cooperate with all review activities.

Initially and periodically, TRUSTe reviews the site and seeds it with personal user information to ensure continued compliance. They also perform periodic conformance reviews with their auditors: PricewaterhouseCoopers, LLP and KPMG Peat Marwick.

The Roots of TRUSTe

TRUSTe grew from an idea during a lecture on trust at Esther Dyson's PC Forum in March 1996. Among the attendees were Lori Fena, executive director of the Electronic Frontier Foundation (EFF), and Charles Jennings, founder and CEO of Portland Software. After the lecture, the two were introduced by a mutual friend who knew that each had espoused the need for branded symbols of trust on the Internet similar to UL Labs or Good Housekeeping "seals of approval." Over the next few months, Fena and Jennings gathered up a small team of interested Internet electronic commerce pioneers, and they met regularly to draw up plans and develop criteria for bringing TRUSTe to the Internet. The group unanimously agreed on two cornerstone principles to govern the TRUSTe program:

1. Users have a right to informed consent.

2. No single privacy principle is adequate for all situations.

The Privacy Partnership

In late 1998, several major TRUSTe objectives were realized when notable Internet portal sites joined with TRUSTe to launch the Privacy Partnership campaign. The Privacy Partnership is a grass-roots consumer education campaign to raise awareness of the privacy issue. At the same time, TRUSTe launched a major Web site redesign, featuring a new identity rooted in "Building a Web You Can Believe In." Accompanying this was a new license agreement, written to incorporate the fair information practices recommended by the FTC and the Department of Commerce. The new agreement also features a Children's Seal and accompanying requirements for children's sites.

For more information, visit the TRUSTe Web Site at: www.truste.org.

Are Seals for Everyone?

As with any policy framework, seal programs are not without their opponents. The same charge that is leveled at seal programs is raised against more "technical" solutions such as P3P: how do you really know that the Web site is doing what its privacy policy says it is doing? Obviously, any time you have a system built by humans, it can be compromised by humans. When you step into a high-rise elevator and read the latest safety inspection report posted above the buttons, how do you know that the inspector really did his job and that the elevator won't go hurtling to the ground floor with you in it?

There are only a couple of guarantees in life, and safe elevators and Web sites aren't on the list. Still, any safety program requires both the trust of the users (as long as that trust continues to be earned) and an unflagging vigilance from the parties involved. P3P and seal programs offer in their own way specific features that the Web site and the consumer must weigh and evaluate. Neither platform is comprehensive or foolproof.

Finally, one aspect of the seal program that its proponents cite as an advantage, namely the use of a third party to monitor and report a Web site's adherence to its privacy policies, is seen as a limitation by its detractors. The latter do not recognize the advantage of paying for accountants to monitor a Web site, especially if the accountants are not familiar with the organization's interests and the policies of the company.

As of this writing, the debate over the World Wide Web Consortium's P3P and seal programs rages on in an attempt to prove that the online industry can self-regulate. Perhaps the threat of greater governmental involvement will help all concerned parties find common ground before that ground is found for them.

Confidence Breeds Confidence

As people demand more in the way of assurances for safety, security, and confidentiality of information, the industry will continue to respond with increasingly better solutions. While efforts like BBBOnline, CPAWebTrust, TRUSTe, and others expand and flourish, the explosive growth of e-commerce that industry experts proclaim might arrive sooner than anyone predicts. If a little bad press goes a long way, just think where a lot of good press will take you!

Third-Party Seals of Privacy Assurance Checklist

In this chapter we covered the importance of having third-party seals of privacy assurance. By now, you should have an understanding of the:

- Purpose and value of a seal program
- Characteristics of a seal program
- Process of obtaining a seal

In addition, we reviewed the different organizations that offer seal programs and their intended audiences.

Keeping Your Policies
Up to Date

In this chapter, you'll learn that privacy is a two-sided issue. It poses challenges for businesses that need the Internet as a vital link in their business strategy while acting as custodian of the data they receive and transmit. Privacy also challenges the individual to take some responsibility for his practices and behavior on the Internet. They should divulge only that information required to complete a task and no more. They should be wary of sites that do not exhibit bona fide privacy policies. For the Internet to succeed as the new model for business strategy, both the business and the consumer must realize that they must strike a partnership and protect their own interests while not stifling the interests of the other party.

You have learned about steps you must take to institute a privacy policy and the importance of doing so. Now you'll learn about the importance of keeping your policy current while being ever mindful of the consumers' privacy concerns.

Understanding the importance of privacy and security measures helps you establish a basis for building trusting relationships with your customer. Making the commitment to honor your privacy policies and comply with accepted practices and regulations will help you earn and keep your customer's confidence. However, initiating a privacy policy is not enough to address the privacy imperative adequately. You need to keep up to date with your policies and practices, keep in touch with the customers' needs and fears, and make sure you are compliant with new legislation. At the end of this chapter, we have a checklist of the top ten things you should be doing to protect the privacy of your users.

In the course of business, one of the biggest temptations companies face is to use customer data and e-mail IDs contrary to their customers' desires, for example by selling them to third parties such as direct marketing firms who are willing to pay handsomely for such information. The Direct Marketers Association (DMA: www.the-dma.org), one of the oldest and largest trade association for users and suppliers in the direct, database and interactive marketing fields, has prepared a Privacy Promise statement that it feels will help businesses maintain the trust of their customers. Their privacy policy, "Privacy Promise to American Consumers," became effective in July 1999 for all DMA member companies. The DMA advocates that members understand, adopt, and enforce the Privacy Promise. The Privacy Promise becomes the *de facto* privacy policy for DMA members, an effort to avert greater federal regulation. The three steps of DMA's Privacy Promise policy follow.

The Privacy Promise Member Compliance Guide

Step 1: Take Responsibility

Designate an executive to be responsible for your organization's compliance with the Privacy Promise. This will help with follow-up communications should there be a privacy issue for your organization to address.

Review the Privacy Promise requirements, and determine how they apply to your organization.

The Promise specifies requirements for B2C marketers performing such functions as:

- Mailing list user

- Mailing list compiler

- Mailing list manager

- Mailing list broker

- Mailing list owner

- Mailing service bureau

- Mailing supplier

Some companies perform all of those functions and, therefore, need to understand the requirements of all functions. The requirements of the Privacy Promise are defined by your relationship to the consumers named on your mailing lists.

Following are the Privacy Promise requirements:

Step 2, Part 1: Notice

If your organization is a B2C marketer that rents, sells, or exchanges lists of customers, you must give your customers notice that they have a choice not to have their contact information rented, sold, or exchanged.

Timing of Notice

The first notice must take place when, or soon after, a "prospect" becomes a "customer."

Definition of "Customer"

A person is defined as a "customer" if that person: bought something from you; donated to you; is identified by you as a "customer" on a list that you rent or exchange with someone else; has inquired about your products, services, or organization; and/or is a sweepstakes entrant (whether or not he or she has purchased).

Definition of "Prospect"

A person is defined as a "prospect" if that person has not previously purchased from or donated to you. For example, a gift recipient is considered a prospect because he or she has not purchased an item or requested information from you.

Annual Notice

You should give follow-up notices at least once a year. (However, if you contact a customer less frequently than once a year, notice need only be given as often as you contact the customer.) A separate communications piece for this notice is not required. You may include the notice in any routine customer communication. It should, however, be easy for the customer to find, read, and understand. Notice is required regardless of the medium you use to contact customers: mail, phone, fax, print, or online. Notice need not be in the same medium as the solicitation, but, again, it must be easy for the customers to find, read, and understand.

List compilers, brokers, owners, and service bureaus must give notice only if they are communicating directly to the customer under their own company or organization name. Otherwise, where they have no direct relationship with the customer, their obligation is to request and encourage marketers to give notice to their customers, and to make list users aware of the Privacy Promise.

Step 2, Part 2: Honoring Opt Out Requests

All consumer marketers must promptly honor individual requests to opt out of the sale, rental, or exchange of their contact information for marketing purposes.

Step 2, Part 3: In-House Suppression

List owners and list users must honor individual requests for no future contact from both customers and prospects.

Companies who wish to provide notice of in-house suppression could use or adapt the following language:

A. If you decide you no longer wish to receive our catalog, send your mailing label with your request to (fill in the blank).

B. We would like to continue sending you information only on those subjects of interest to you. If you don't wish to continue to receive information on any of the following product lines, just let us know by (fill in the blank).

C. If you would like to receive our catalog less frequently, let us know by (fill in the blank).

Step 2, Part 4: Use of the DMA Mail, Telephone, and E-Mail Preference Services

Marketers who contact consumers are required to use Mail Preference Service (MPS), Telephone Preference Service (TPS), or e-Mail Preference Service (EMPS), voluntary self-regulatory mechanisms set up by the DMA to enable consumers to opt out of receiving unsolicited sales and marketing calls for all consumer marketing campaigns. Direct marketers are not required to use MPS/TPS/EMPS on their own customer files before contacting their own customers.

The list user is the one responsible for using MPS/TPS before soliciting prospects. Usage of the mechanism by either the list owner or the list user, however, will satisfy the requirement of these self-regulatory mechanisms. The goal is to ensure that the prospect's decision not to receive mail and telephone solicitations is respected. List owners and users may wish to specify whose obligation it is in the list rental contract. For example, a list owner or manager may require by contractual obligation that a list user must use MPS/TPS.

An example of contract language specifying MPS/TPS responsibility follows:

"[List User] hereby acknowledges and agrees that as a condition of using [List Owner's] list, in accordance with the terms and conditions of this Agreement, [List User] will, prior to such use, remove, and refrain from contacting all names that appear on The DMA's MPS and TPS files except those individuals that are already a customer of [List User]."

Although list brokers and managers are not the parties responsible for using MPS/TPS, DMA members who are list brokers and managers must advocate their use to business partners and clients. List brokers and managers could fulfill this requirement by including a paragraph encouraging this use in their sales material.

Step 3: Take the Pledge

Figure 10-1 shows the pledge that the DMA requests that users and suppliers of mailing lists take when they're prepared to honor the Privacy Promise.

What Happens if a DMA Member Does Not Follow the Privacy Promise?

If the DMA Committee on Ethical Business Practice determines that a member appears not to be in compliance with the Privacy Promise, the company will be contacted and asked for immediate compliance. The member will then need to come into immediate

Figure 10-1   The DMA Marketer's Pledge

Privacy Promise Member Compliance Guide

Step Three: Take The Pledge

Consumer Marketer's Promise

I certify that my company:
(please initial)

Provides customers with notice of their ability to
opt out of information rental, sale or exchange.   ———

Honors customer opt out requests not to have
their contact information transferred to others for marketing purposes.   ———

Honors consumer requests for in-house
suppress to stop receiving solicitations from our company.   ———

Uses The DMA Preference Service suppression
files, which now exist for mail and telephone lists - and will soon exist for e-mail lists. ———

Supplier's Promise

I certify that my company:
(please initial)

Encourages our Consumer Marketer customers to comply with
The DMA Privacy Promise _____

Business to Business, Resident/Occupant, International

I certify that my company is exempted from the Privacy Promise _____

This certifies that the below named company is
in full compliance with the Privacy Promise, as described
in the Privacy Promise Member Compliance Guide, receipt
of which is hereby acknowledged. By my signature, I
certify that I have personally reviewed the company's
practices that are subject to the Privacy Promise, and
that I am my company's designated contact authorized to
make this certification of compliance on behalf of the
below named company.

Signed: _____ Date: _____

Title: _____

Company Name: _____

Please Print

Name: _____ E-Mail Address: _____

Address: _____City/State/Zip: _____

Phone Number: _____ Fax Number: _____

Please complete and send to the

Direct Marketing Association,
Attn: Privacy Promise
1111 19th Street, NW, Washington, DC 20036-3603;
or Fax to 202.955.0085.

Reproduced with permission of DMA.

compliance and/or demonstrate to the Committee that its practices are consistent with the Privacy Promise.

Any unanswered Committee question or unmet Committee request will be referred to the DMA board for appropriate action, which may include censure, suspension, or expulsion from the DMA, and publicity to that effect.

For additional information about the DMA Privacy Promise, visit the DMA Web site at *www.dma.org.*

Step into Your Customers' Shoes

Businesses that successfully develop sound privacy policies do so in part because they anticipate the concerns and the needs of the individual. Understanding the strategies of privacy advocacy groups such as the Center for Democracy and Technology (CDT) will assist you with this task. The CDT has prepared a list of the top ten ways online users can protect their privacy. By keeping in mind the kinds of things a customer is looking for on your site, you can reduce the risks of losing customers or employees. The more you can meet their needs for security and privacy, the likelier you'll build—and maintain—longstanding and rewarding relationships.

The Top Ten Ways to Protect Privacy Online

1. **Look for privacy policies on the Web.** Web sites can collect a lot of information about a consumer's visit—what computer they are using, what type of hardware and software they have, what Web sites they have visited. Web sites that ask the consumer

to provide even a small amount of personal information can easily tie the data they provide to his browsing habits.

When a consumer goes to a Web site that has no privacy policy, they are encouraged to write and tell the company that they are a user of their site, their privacy is important to them, and they would like to see them post a policy. The CDT has developed the Privacy Watchdog (www.cdt.org) site to guide the consumer through this process. The user answers a series of seven yes/no questions about privacy policy practices at the Web sites they visit. The Privacy Watchdog generates a letter that the user may edit and send to a Web site. The letter may praise or criticize a site's privacy practices depending on the user's responses to the seven questions.

An increasing number of Web sites have privacy policies that detail the sites' information practices. The consumer is encouraged to look for these policies and read them carefully. While privacy statements are not the only answer to online privacy risks, the consumer is generally encouraged and commended to do so.

2. **Get a separate e-mail account for personal e-mail.** Often, online users do not realize that e-mail sent from their work accounts is open to their employers. If an employee sends an e-mail from his home, and they are using their work e-mail server, even then they are most likely storing a copy of his note on their employer's main computer server. Their boss has a legal right to read any and all correspondence in this account or on their work computer at any time.

Getting a separate account for personal use allows the user to check his personal messages without using their workplace e-mail server. Some private accounts can be configured to enable them to check their personal mail from work without downloading it onto the company computer.

3. **Teach kids that giving out personal information online means giving it to strangers.** Teach children that they need your permission before they can give out their name, address, or other information about themselves or the family. Several years ago, a number of Web sites encouraged children to give information about themselves or their family; some enticed kids with games and free gifts. In 1998, a law was passed requiring companies to gain parental consent before collecting personal information from children under thirteen years old. If a parent or other concerned adult is concerned about a Web site collecting information from children without consent, he is encouraged to contact the FTC at kidsprivacy@ftc.gov.

4. **Clear memory cache after browsing.** After a user browses the Web, copies of all accessed pages and images are saved on the computer's memory. While these copies make subsequent visits to the same sites faster, the browsing record has grave implications for personal privacy, particularly if the user shares a computer or browser at work. They can delete most of their online trail by simply going to the "Preferences" folder in his browser and clicking on the "Empty Cache" button. Sometimes this option is in the "Advanced" menu of the browser preferences. In Internet Explorer, the user should go to "Internet Options" from the "Tools" menu and click on "Clear History."

5. **Make sure that online forms are secure.** Online forms may be digitally transported in ways that leave them vulnerable to undesired access. Alternatively, online forms may be encrypted so

that only the intended recipients can readily translate the information. Ensuring that user information is stored and transferred in secure ways is one of the keys to protecting his privacy. Fortunately, browser companies have realized the importance of data security; newer browsers are designed to indicate whether the accessed page allows encrypted transfers. The commonly used graphics are a key, which is broken if the page is unsecure, and a lock—locked means secure and unlocked means not secure. The graphic appears in the corner of the browser screen; clicking on the lock or the key will inform the user of additional security information about the page. They should not input sensitive personal information about themself (such as financial or medical data) on Web pages that are not secure.

6. **Reject unnecessary cookies.** Cookies enable Web sites to store information about a user's visit on their hard drive. Cookies inform site operators if the user has visited the site and, if they have obtained a username and password, cookies remember that information for them. Many of the "personalized" search engines use cookies to deliver news topics that a user selects; sites often use these same preferences to target advertisement. Furthermore, sites use cookies to track a user's online behavior and create a profile without the user realizing it.

7. **Use anonymous remailers.** Anonymity is essential to privacy and free speech. It protects whistle blowers and writers of controversial material; most simply, it may enable one to publish without a forwarding address. The e-mail technology creates problems for the right to anonymous communication because the sender of a message can be traced back through digital paths.

Created to address privacy risks and concerns, "anonymous remailers" presently allow a user to send anonymous e-mail messages.

A joint project of the George Mason Society and the Global Internet Liberty Campaign created one very good remailer available on the Web at: www.gilc.org/speech/anonymous/remailer.html.

8. **Encrypting e-mail.** E-mail is not as secure a medium as many believe!

Unintended third parties can easily reroute and read e-mail; messages are often saved for indefinite periods of time. Presently, there exist technologies that allow the user to encrypt their messages in order to protect their privacy. Some e-mail programs (i.e., Internet Explorer Outlook and Netscape Messenger) have encryption. Pretty Good Privacy (PGP), a popular encryption software, is free for noncommercial use. The user can read more on PGP and download the encryption software at http://web.mit.edu/network/pgp.html.

9. **Use anonymizers while browsing.** From the moment a user types in a Web address, a log records information about his visit.

Every day, most of us walk down the street without being recognized or tracked. Whereas anonymity is often taken for granted in the physical world, such luxury is not available online. Tools that strip out user information, thus preserving anonymity, have already been created; a few are readily available on the net. Visit http://www.freedom.net and http://www.anonymizer.com.

10. **Opt out of third-party informationsharing.** Many online companies provide the user with the option to get off (or opt out) the lists that share your information. Some companies enable users to easily opt out—users are often able to do so online. A number of companies go a step further and ask the user's permission (opt in) before sharing personal information that they have

collected. Often, however, companies make opting out difficult or virtually impossible: addresses are buried, one cannot opt-out on-line, etc. CDT has created Operation Opt-Out to help you control how a user's personal data is collected and distributed.

Extra! Use common sense. Reading the Top Ten list—as well as encountering multiple news stories that portray Web companies as charlatans or worse—can instill paranoia even in the most fear-less Web user. The user must realize, however, that people in cy-berspace are the same people he encounters every day in the phys-ical reality: his neighbors, his colleagues. Using many of the same behavior patterns that he uses in the offline environment will take him a long way toward protecting himself online. The CDT asks the user to repeat a set of questions when he is online: Would he give his credit card number to a street vendor? Would he transact business with a well-established, trusted firm? How much infor-mation does the newspaper realistically need to process a sub-scription? Will he be subjected to a ton of unsolicited mail if he discloses his physical or e-mail address? From the business per-spective this question becomes: Are you, the business owner, col-lecting more information about the user than you really need?

The CDT asks the user to apply common sense, ask ques-tions, and seek out resources. As users become more attuned to privacy issues and how their personal data could be used, they will become increasingly demanding in knowing a site's privacy pol-icy. The astute business owner will anticipate the user's concerns, and address them with sound policies and practices such as those advocated by many organizations such as we have described in this book.

The Frontier of Privacy

Stepping into the new millennium, we ask ourselves, "Was George Orwell off base with his visions of a 1984 Big Brother society, or was he simply wrong about his timing?"

The jury is still out, deliberating over the direction of privacy preservation. Can we continue with business as usual and *laissez-faire* attitudes from the U.S. government, or will regulations squeeze out all but the most tenacious? Will we continue to tolerate rampant abuses of privacy, or will boycotts of new age technology spell doom for an otherwise promising medium?

Throughout this book you have learned about privacy problems, pending laws, policies, processes, and technologies to mitigate concerns, and you have seen a variety of examples from companies and organizations that truly respect privacy as something more than a buzzword.

In pulling out our somewhat clouded crystal ball to try and find the trends in the industry, we're clearly headed in the direction of some governance of privacy that will likely be too intrusive for some businesses and too lax for certain privacy advocacy groups. However, without doing anything, and as long as someone out there with a sufficient market share continues to use customer personal information without respect to its source or accuracy, we continue remaining at risk and law enforcement becomes more likely.

The FTC isn't apt to wait for another five years of reports to Congress before clamping down and turning privacy and security measures from a good idea into the privacy imperative. With the information you have collected throughout this book, you should be well on your way to understanding the current privacy landscape and creating your own privacy policies. Chances are, we will continue to see sector-specific privacy policy and legislation before we see a comprehensive national policy on privacy. For example, we are already seeing laws that address privacy issues in the financial and health care industries. A brief description of some of the more important federal legislation follows. (Bear in mind that the 107th Congress currently has fifty bills before it, everything from the Student Privacy Protection Act to the Law Enforcement Officers Privacy Protection act, all of which you can read about in detail at http://thomas.loc.gov/ [Thomas Legislative Information On the Internet]).

Banking Privacy Laws Take Effect

On 13 November 2000, the Financial Privacy Rule took effect. The law, entitled the "Privacy of Consumer Financial Information Rule," implements the privacy provisions of the Gramm-Leach-Bliley Act of 1999.

The rule requires banks and other financial institutions to provide consumers with clear and conspicuous notice of privacy practices and the opportunity to opt out of the disclosure of their "nonpublic personal information" to nonaffiliated third parties. This law is intended to address some of the cross-sell concerns as conglomerates buy up banks, insurance companies, and securities brokerage houses in attempts to provide a one-stop shop for all matters financial.

Health Insurance Portability and Accountability Act

In 1996, Congress enacted the Health Insurance Portability and Accountability Act (HIPAA) after recognizing the need to control the electronic transmission of patient information. In the past, family doctors, hospitals, and pharmacists kept patient information locked away in file cabinets. Today, the storage and transmission of this information using computer systems controlled only by a patchwork of state laws called for a more comprehensive and secure safeguard of patient health information; hence, the 1996 HIPPA Act.

Congress had until August 1999 to pass comprehensive health privacy legislation. When they failed to do so, the Department of Health and Human Services (HHS) received the task. In November 1999, the HHS proposed privacy regulations and called for comments on their proposals. After several revisions to the act, the HHS passed a revised HIPPA Act in April 2001 that includes the following consumer privacy protections:

• **Patient Education on Privacy Protections.** Medical plans and health-care providers must disclose to the patient how they use and disclose health information.

• **Access to Medical Records.** Patients are able to obtain, review, and amend their medical records.

• **Patient Consent.** Plans and providers must obtain the patient's approval before sharing treatment, payment, or related information with others. Patients must authorize on a separate form nonroutine disclosure of their information.

• **Complaint Procedure.** Patients will have a procedure to follow in case they want to file a complaint or grievance against a plan or health care provider, or with the HHS.

Chief Privacy Officers on the Scene

New government regulations and legislation pending at home and abroad have been sparked by rising consumer concerns and a business environment that leapfrogs over itself almost daily and questions whether or not any of the old rules still apply.

This has compelled businesses to address privacy in new ways. One of those ways is to designate a company officer whose main function is to oversee and coordinate all of the organization's activities with privacy implications.

In the fall of 2000, *Computerworld* magazine reported the rise of chief privacy officers (CPOs) within corporate America. This relatively new trend establishes a role within the executive office to help ensure that privacy promises are maintained and kept.

Ronald Hoffman, the privacy issues manager at Mutual of Omaha Insurance Co., told *Computerworld*, "Privacy is something that is going to help build a trusting relationship with our customers that we hope will allow us to retain their business and acquire new business."

To help advance the development of CPO roles within corporations, the Association of Corporate Privacy Officers (ACPO) was launched in September 2000 as an outgrowth of Privacy & American Business' CPO 2000 Program headed by Dr. Alan F. Westin, described by the *Wall Street Journal* as "the keenest observer of public attitudes toward privacy in the 20th century."[1] Westin feels that every "sensible" company will include a CPO on its management team. To this end, the CPO hopes to develop a

---

1. As quoted in "Privacy and American Business," www.pandab.org/cpo2001/acpo.html.

pool of well-trained privacy officers from which companies who understand the importance of privacy issues may draw.

Founding Members of ACPO's Organizing Committee include privacy officers from:

- American Express

- Dun & Bradstreet

- Go.com

- Nationwide Insurance

- EDS

- PriceWaterhouseCoopers

- Equifax

- Image Data

- Citigroup

- Mutual of Omaha

- Bell Atlantic

- Delta Airlines

- Royal Bank

- Sabre, Inc

- Studio Legale Imperiale

Westin's sentiment is echoed by Peter Swire, formerly President Clinton's privacy czar, and Microsoft's CPO, Richard

Purcell, both of whom emphasize the importance of the role of the CPO as corporations take a more active stance on privacy.

Members of ACPO also are entitled to other benefits, including:

- Corporate privacy officer certification

- Professional recognition from other members for leadership and/or accomplishments in the privacy field

- Networking opportunities with peers

- Salary benchmarks

- Templates for job descriptions

- Information on placement of the CPO within the corporate structure

ACPO offers its members opportunities and activities directed at helping them master the rapidly evolving field of consumer privacy and data protection and find practical solutions. ACPO also provides members with education and training to give them the practical strategies and techniques they need to handle such issues and challenges. ACPO serves as a clearinghouse of privacy-related information, apprising members of the latest news and trends in the corporate privacy field through ACPO publications, e-communications, and through the maintenance of the ACPO Web site at www.corporateprivacyofficers.org. You may consider joining ACPO to help advance their causes.

New Frontiers, New Problems

We close with what we feel is our "Top Ten" list of initiatives that any business concerned about privacy should be taking now (if you aren't already doing so):

1.   Review your current privacy policies. Are they sufficient to address the concerns of your customers? If not, determine if you have the resources in-house to create your policies; if not, consider looking for outside help.

2.   Educate your employees about the importance of privacy matters both to the customer and the company.

3.   Understand current and pending state and federal privacy legislation that might affect your operation. Vigilance is the byword here.

4.   Consider hiring a CPO if your organization is large enough and can afford what should be a highly visible management position.

5.   Review the security of your systems. Privacy is not just about policy and legislation. It also means protecting your data from both internal and external threats.

6.   "Mystery shop" on your own site by planting data about fictitious customers with mailing addresses and e-mail IDs that you can monitor to see if information leakage is occurring.

7.   Keep up with international laws that may affect your business, including the Safe Harbor provisions and OECD directives for information privacy and security.

8.   Subscribe to consumer protection services (like

BBBOnline), and join organizations that focus on consumer issues related to privacy.

9. Participate in seal programs to help assure your customers that you're serious about their privacy concerns.

10. Because technology won't stand still, revisit each of these steps at least annually to maintain a strong privacy posture.

The world of Winston Smith in Orwell's *1984* may not have come to pass, but certainly the issue of privacy looms large in the minds of the consumer. We have seen an issue once the domain of Cold War politics, government spies, and political infiltration move into the world of consumerism. Perhaps it will be here that the privacy issue will gather its force and unleash itself unless businesses listen to the concerns of the public and respond to them through sound and thoughtful privacy policy that the consumer can easily understand. Money talks, and if it learns that it is being listened to unannounced, it may just stop talking.

APPENDIXES

FTC Privacy Policy
Development Guidelines

This appendix lists the guidelines for companies developing their own privacy policies, as recommended by the FTC.

1. Organizations establishing privacy policies should incorporate the elements of the widely accepted Code of Fair Information Practice:

    a. The existence of all data systems with personal information in them should be publicly disclosed, and the purpose for which information is gathered about people should be disclosed. This is the principle of openness or transparency.

    b. There must be a way for an individual to find out what information about themself is in a record and how it is used.

    c. There must be a way for an individual to prevent information about themself that was obtained for one purpose (which was stated when the information was gathered) from being used or made available, either within the organization or outside, for a purpose that is incompatible with the original purpose, without getting the consent of the individual. This is the principle of secondary use.

d.   There must be a way for an individual to correct or amend a record that contains information that is identifiable to themself.

e.   The organization creating, maintaining, using, or disseminating records of identifiable personal data must ensure the reliability, accuracy, security, and timeliness of the data. In other words, the custodian of information that is disseminated has an obligation to the individual to make sure it is accurate, secure, and not misused. This obligation ought not be delegated to another entity.

2.   An organization must make sure that other entities handling personal information on behalf of the first organization are bound by these same principles.

3.   An organization must conduct periodic risk assessments, balancing the possibility or probability of unauthorized access or disclosure against the cost of security precautions and the expected effectiveness of the precautions. In some cases, it will be necessary to establish an audit trail so that records are kept of disclosures of personal information, both within the organization and outside.

4.   Organizations must take special precautions in collecting and using personal information about children, both those thirteen years or younger and those eighteen years or younger.

5.   An organization should openly disclose its policies and practices with regard to electronic surveillance of its employees'

and customers' telephone calls, e-mail, Internet usage, changing rooms, and rest rooms. It must articulate in advance the reasons for the surveillance.

6. An organization should collect only that personal information that is proportional to the purpose of the information. It must scrutinize each demand for information to determine that it is relevant and necessary.

7. An organization should designate an individual or office (whether full-time or part-time) to handle privacy issues by (a) acting as an ombudsman for customers or employees, (b) assessing the privacy impact of new undertakings, (c) ensuring that the organization complies with all laws and trade-association standards, and (d) informing the organization of the latest technology and policies that affect the privacy of customers or employees. An organization, if it utilizes "opt out" for customers to refrain from certain uses of their information, should make exercising "opt out" easy, as easy as clicking a button or checking a box, without the need to write a letter or communicate with another office.

8. An organization should conduct periodic training of its employees (and volunteers) to ensure that they know (a) applicable laws on confidentiality that govern the organization, (b) the organization's policies and actual practices, (c) the rationale for protecting confidentiality and the sensitivity of personal information, and (d) the ability to recognize possible breaches and to report them to the proper person. An organization may choose to certify that employees who handle personal information are properly trained.

TRUSTe Model
Privacy Statement

Appendix B shows the TRUSTe Model Privacy Statement from the TRUSTe Resource Guide found at www.truste. org/bus/pub_resourceguide.html. The site consists of (a) the Model Privacy Statement and (b) a site coordinator's guide.

The TRUSTe Resource Guide is aimed at helping you get started on your Web site's privacy statement.

The Model Privacy Statement is an example of the right way to draft a privacy statement given a specific business model. TRUSTe has taken out the company name and other unique corporate identifiers to enable this document to be used as a starting point and must be edited according to your site's specific privacy practices.

Sample Privacy Policy

This confirms that [COMPANY X] is a licensee of the TRUSTe Privacy Program. This privacy statement discloses the privacy practices for [URL of COMPANY X WEBSITE].

TRUSTe is an independent, non-profit organization the mission of which is to build users' trust and confidence in the Internet by promoting the use of fair information practices. Because this Web site wants to demonstrate its commitment to your privacy, it has agreed to disclose its information practices and have its privacy practices reviewed for compliance by TRUSTe. By displaying the TRUSTe trustmark, this Web site has agreed to notify you of:

1. What personally identifiable information of yours or third party personally identification is collected from you through the Web site

2. The organization collecting the information

3. How the information is used

4. With whom the information may be shared

5. What choices are available to you regarding collection, use, and distribution of the information

6. The kind of security procedures that are in place to protect the loss, misuse, or alteration of information under [NAME OF COMPANY] control

7. How you can correct any inaccuracies in the information

If you feel that this company is not abiding by its posted privacy policy, you should first contact [INSERT NAME OF INDIVID-

UAL, DEPARTMENT OR GROUP RESPONSIBLE FOR IN-QUIRIES] by [INSERT CONTACT INFORMATION; E-MAIL, PHONE, POSTAL MAIL, ETC.] If you do not receive acknowl-edgment of your inquiry or your inquiry has not been satisfacto-rily addressed, you should then contact TRUSTe at *http://www.truste.org*. TRUSTe will then serve as a liaison with the Web site to resolve your concerns.

Information Collection and Use

Company X is the sole owner of the information collected on this site. We will not sell, share, or rent this information to others in ways different from what is disclosed in this statement. Company X collects information from our users at several differ-ent points on our Web site.

Registration

In order to use this Web site, a user must first complete the regis-tration form. During registration a user is required to give his or her contact information (such as name and e-mail address). This information is used to contact the user about the services on our site for which they have expressed interest. It is optional for the user to provide demographic information (such as income level and gender) and unique identifiers (such as social security num-ber), but encouraged so we can provide a more personalized ex-perience on our site.

Order

We request information from the user on our order form. Here a user must provide contact information (such as name and shipping address) and financial information (such as credit card number, expiration date). This information is used for billing purposes and to fill customers' orders. If we have trouble processing an order, this contact information is used to get in touch with the user.

Cookies

A cookie is a piece of data stored on the user's hard drive containing information about the user. Usage of a cookie is in no way linked to any personally identifiable information while on our site. Once the user closes their browser, the cookie simply terminates. For instance, by setting a cookie on our site, the user would not have to log in a password more than once, thereby saving time while on our site. If a user rejects the cookie, they may still use our site. The only drawback to this is that the user will be limited in some areas of our site. For example, the user will not be able to participate in any of our sweepstakes, contests, or monthly drawings that take place. Cookies can also enable us to track and target the interests of our users to enhance their experience on our site.

Some of our business partners use cookies on our site (for example, advertisers). However, we have no access to or control over these cookies.

Log Files

We use IP addresses to analyze trends, administer the site, track users' movements, and gather broad demographic information for aggregate use. IP addresses are not linked to personally identifiable information.

Sharing

We will share aggregated demographic information with our partners and advertisers. This is not linked to any personal information that can identify any individual person.

We use an outside shipping company to ship orders, and a credit card processing company to bill users for goods and services. These companies do not retain, share, store, or use personally identifiable information for any secondary purposes.

We partner with another party to provide specific services. When the user signs up for these services, we will share names or other contact information that is necessary for the third party to provide these services.

These parties are not allowed to use personally identifiable information except for the purpose of providing these services.

Links

This Web site contains links to other sites. Please be aware that we [COMPANY X] are not responsible for the privacy practices of such other sites. We encourage our users to be aware when they leave our site and to read the privacy statements of each and every Web site that collects personally identifiable information. This privacy statement applies solely to information collected by this Web site.

Newsletter

If a user wishes to subscribe to our newsletter, we ask for contact information such as name and e-mail address.

Surveys and Contests

From time to time our site requests information from users via surveys or contests. Participation in these surveys or contests is completely voluntary and the user therefore has a choice of whether or not to disclose this information. Information requested may include contact information (such as name and shipping address) and demographic information (such as ZIP code, age level).

Contact information will be used to notify the winners and award prizes. Survey information will be used for purposes of monitoring or improving the use and satisfaction of this site.

Tell-a-Friend

If a user elects to use our referral service for informing a friend about our site, we ask them for the friend's name and e-mail address. [COMPANY X] will automatically send the friend a one-time e-mail inviting them to visit the site. [COMPANY X] stores this information for the sole purpose of sending this one-time e-mail. The friend may contact [COMPANY X] at [INSERT URL] to request the removal of this information from their database.

Security

This Web site takes every precaution to protect our users' information. When users submit sensitive information via the Web site, your information is protected both online and offline.

When our registration/order form asks users to enter sensitive information (such as credit card number and/or social security number), that information is encrypted and is protected with the best encryption software in the industry—SSL. While on a secure page, such as our order form, the lock icon on the bottom of Web browsers such as Netscape Navigator and Microsoft Internet Explorer becomes locked, as opposed to unlocked, or open, when you are just "surfing." To learn more about SSL, follow this link [INSERT LINK].

While we use SSL encryption to protect sensitive information online, we also do everything in our power to protect user information off-line. All of our users' information, not just the sensitive information mentioned above, is restricted in our offices. Only employees who need the information to perform a specific job (for example, our billing clerk or a customer service representative) are granted access to personally identifiable information. Our employees must use password-protected screen-savers when they leave their desks. When they return, they must reenter their password to regain access to your information. Furthermore, all employees are kept up to date on our security and privacy practices. Every quarter, as well as any time new policies are added, our employees are notified and/or reminded about the importance we place on privacy, and what they can do to ensure our customers' information is protected. Finally, the servers on which we store personally identifiable information are kept in a secure environment, behind a locked cage.

If you have any questions about the security at our Web site, you can send an e-mail to security@thiswebsite.com.

Supplementation of Information

In order for this Web site to properly fulfill its obligation to our customers, it is necessary for us to supplement the information we receive with information from third-party sources.

For example, to determine if our customers qualify for one of our credit cards, we use their name and social security number to

request a credit report. Once we determine a user's credit-worthi-
ness, this document is destroyed.

(or)

In order for this Web site to enhance its ability to tailor the site
to an individual's preference, we combine information about the
purchasing habits of users with similar information from our partners, Company Y and Company Z, to create a personalized user
profile. When a user makes a purchase from either of these two
companies, the companies collect and share that purchase information with us so we can tailor the site to our users' preferences.

Special Offers

We send all new members a welcoming e-mail to verify password
and username. Established members will occasionally receive information on products, services, special deals, and a newsletter.
Out of respect for the privacy of our users we present the option
to not receive these types of communications. Please see our
choice and opt out option below.

Site and Service Updates

We also send the user site and service announcement updates.
Members are not able to unsubscribe from service announcements, which contain important information about the service.
We communicate with the user to provide requested services and
in regards to issues relating to their account via e-mail or phone.

Correction/Updating Personal Information

If a user's personally identifiable information changes (such as
your ZIP code), or if a user no longer desires our service, we will

endeavor to provide a way to correct, update, or remove that user's personal data provided to us. This can usually be done at the member information page or by e-mailing customer support. [Some sites may also provide telephone or postal mail options for updating or correcting personal information].

Choice/Opt-Out

Our users are given the opportunity to "opt out" of having their information used for purposes not directly related to our site at the point where we ask for the information. For example, our order form has an "opt out" mechanism so users who buy a product from us, but don't want to receive any marketing material, can keep their e-mail address off of our lists.

Users who no longer wish to receive our newsletter or promotional materials from our partners may opt out of receiving these communications by replying with "unsubscribe" in the e-mail's subject line or by e-mailing us at support@thiswebsite.com. [Some sites are able to offer opt out mechanisms on member information pages and also supply a telephone or postal option as a way to opt out.]

Users of our site are always notified when their information is being collected by any outside parties. We do this so our users can make an informed choice as to whether or not they should proceed with services that require an outside party.

Notification of Changes

If we decide to change our privacy policy, we will post those changes on our home page so our users are always aware of what information we collect, how we use it, and under which circumstances, if any, we disclose it. If at any point we decide to use personally identifiable information in a manner different from that stated at the time it was collected, we will notify users by way of an e-mail. Users will have a choice as to whether or not we use their information in this different manner. We will use information in accordance with the privacy policy under which the information was collected.

Privacy Advocates

Government regulators are becoming increasingly anxious to impose laws to mandate strict compliance with sound information-handling practices. By reading this book you've started down the right road to performing your part. At this point you're left with a vast array of tools, technologies, and services that you'll find helpful along the way to creating and implementing an effective e-privacy program. With action on your part now, you can stay ahead of the curve, so when the regulations come you'll be spending your time doing what you do best—making more money on the Internet.

Even though everything may be in place, verified as correctly done, and stamped with the seal of distinguished privacy practices, there's still the matter of maintenance. The world is changing all the time, leaving you with little choice but to change with it. As your site evolves and as you add new services or offerings, your policies—and resultant activities—must continue to adapt to these changes, while remaining compliant with the law and spirit of your e-privacy policy. This will indeed take some work on your part, but thankfully, you're not alone.

In this appendix you'll find a variety of organizations and public interest groups to help you guard against privacy and computer security abuses. Some of the following groups are consumer advocates who believe that stricter government controls are needed because industry is unable or unwilling to self-regulate. Other groups believe that less, not more, government intervention is required and that excessive government regulation will stifle growth of e-commerce and the Internet. Regardless of where your privacy beliefs lie, it behooves you to stay current with the ongoing debate and with state and federal privacy legislation so that you aren't caught with your proverbial "pants down."

Privacy Organizations

American Civil Liberties Union (ACLU)

The ACLU is a national civil liberties organization, founded in 1920. The ACLU conducts extensive litigation on constitutional issues, including privacy and free speech. The ACLU Washington office lobbies Congress on civil liberties and civil rights issues. Their influence in shaping the modern political stance on protecting personal privacy is a driving force in legislative activity. Keeping an eye on their public activity in privacy issues should keep you abreast of imminent changes that may affect your e-commerce practices.

ACLU Web site: www.aclu.org

BBBOnline (BBBO)

The BBBO, is a wholly owned subsidiary of the Council of Better Business Bureaus. Its purpose is to promote trust and confidence on the Internet through reliability and privacy programs. BBBOnline's privacy seal carries the high name recognition that people have grown to trust, and participating in their programs for both traditional e-commerce sites—and those that specialize in children's interests—should help you to attract even the most reluctant online consumers.

BBBOnline Web site: www.bbbonline.com

Center for Democracy and Technology (CDT)

The CDT works to promote democratic values and constitutional liberties in the digital age. With expertise in law, technology, and policy, CDT seeks practical solutions to enhance free expression and privacy in global communications technologies. CDT is dedicated to building consensus among all parties by balancing the needs for individuals to preserve their privacy along with the needs of businesses and government regulators who take an active interest in the future of the Internet and other new communications media. Keeping an eye on their activity, as well as participating in their public forums, may help you in the long run to have a say in the overall scheme of Internet communications.

CDT Web site: www.cdt.org

Electronic Frontier Foundation (EFF)

The EFF was formed in 1990 to maintain and enhance intellectual freedom, privacy, and other values of civil liberties and democracy in networked communications. They publish newsletters, Internet guidebooks, and other documents, provide mailing lists and other online forums, and host a large electronic document archive. The EFF strives to protect the rights of "netizens" worldwide to remain anonymous (if they choose), to prevent using cookies or other tracking mechanisms on unaware users, and free-speech rights to eliminate widespread censorship. As a business participant in their activities, you can gain a voice in their advisory roles for influencing court cases and ultimately in pending legislation.

EFF Web site: www.eff.org

Electronic Privacy Information Center (EPIC)

EPIC is a public interest research center in Washington, DC. It was established in 1994 to focus public attention on emerging civil liberties issues and to protect privacy, the First Amendment, and constitutional values. EPIC is a project of the Fund for Constitutional Government. It works in association with Privacy International, an international human rights group based in London, UK (see below) and is also a member of the Global Internet Liberty Campaign, the Internet Free Expression Alliance, the Internet Privacy Coalition, and the Trans Atlantic Consumer Dialogue (TACD). EPIC conducts litigation, sponsors conferences, produces reports, publishes the *EPIC Alert*, and leads campaigns on privacy issues. Staying up-to-date on EPIC's activities will help you to meet international and legal requirements for electronic privacy on your e-commerce sites.

EPIC Web site: www.epic.org

Junkbusters

Junkbusters is a privacy advocacy group that helps consumers get rid of junk messages such as spam, junk mail, telemarketing calls, etc. It is a for-profit organization that works with trade organizations, governments, public information groups, and corporations to better privacy protection and greater privacy protection for the individual.

Junkbusters Web site: www.junkbusters.com

Online Privacy Alliance (OPA)

The OPA leads and supports self-regulatory initiatives that create an environment of trust and to foster the protection of individuals' privacy online and with electronic commerce.
   The OPA will:

   • Identify and advance effective online privacy policies across the private sector.

   • Support and foster the development and use of self-regulatory enforcement mechanisms and activities, as well as user empowerment technology tools, designed to protect individuals' privacy.

   • Support compliance with and strong enforcement of applicable laws and regulations.

   • Support and foster the development and use of practices and policies that protect the privacy of children.

   • Promote broad awareness of and participation in Alliance initiatives by businesses, nonprofits, policy makers, and consumers; and seek input and support for Alliance initiatives from consumer, business, academic, advocacy, and other organizations that share its commitment to privacy protection.

OPA Web site: www.privacyalliance.org

Organization for Economic Co-operation and Development (OECD)

The OECD consists of 29 member nations that discuss, develop, and perfect economic and social policies. The OECD's work in these areas is directed toward promoting an internationally coordinated approach to policy making in the areas of information security and the protection of privacy on global networks.

In the context of the OECD's work on the global information society and electronic commerce, the Group of Experts on Information Security and Privacy examines issues related to building trust in information and communication networks and electronic commerce, particularly in the areas of:

- Protection of privacy and personal data
- Authentication and Certification
- Cryptography policy
- Security of information systems

OECD Web site: www.oecd.org

Pew Internet and the American Life Project (PIALP)

The PIALP is a nonprofit initiative of the Pew Research Center for People and the Press. The organization creates and funds research of academic caliber that explores the impact of the Internet on children, families, communities, the workplace, schools, etc., exploring its effects upon society in a timely and impartial manner.

Pew Internet Web site: www.pewinternet.org

Privacy Forum (PFM)

The PFM, created in 1992 by Lauren Weinstein, is a moderated e-mail digest for the discussion of privacy issues, telecommunications, data collection, and data sharing. The Forum is a source of information to both individuals and organizations who are concerned about these issues, especially with how the needs of business and other organizations compete with those of the individual.

Privacy Forum Web site: www.vortex.com/privacy

Privacy Foundation (PF)

The PF, based at the University of Denver, was created by Peter Barton, formerly the president of the Cable Value Network (which became the QVC Shopping Network), as an independent watchdog group to guard consumer privacy. Unlike other consumer privacy groups that focus on public policy, the PF concentrates on technology, modeling itself after the Computer Emergency Response Team (CERT) that issues alerts and guidelines when it detects computer security threats.

Privacy Foundation Web site: www.privacyfoundation.org

Privacy International (PI)

PI is an international human rights group based in London, England with offices in Washington, DC, and Sydney, Australia.

PI has members in over 40 countries and has led campaigns against national ID cards, video surveillance, and other privacy violations in numerous countries including Australia, New Zealand, the United Kingdom, and the Philippines. PI publishes the International Privacy Bulletin and sponsors yearly international conferences on privacy issues.

Privacy International Web site: www.privacyinternational.org

Security Advisories

Computer Emergency Response Team (CERT)

The Software Engineering Institute (SEI) is a federally funded research and development center sponsored by the U.S. Department of Defense. SEI is operated at Carnegie Mellon University and is staffed by technical and administrative professionals from government, industry, and academia. One of SEI's primary projects is the Computer Emergency Response Team Coordination Center, or CERT, which serves as the authoritative source for networked systems vulnerabilities and threats.

Networked Systems Survivability

The Networked Systems Survivability Program is based on the experience of CERT to counter intrusions into computer systems connected to the Internet. Based on this experience, SEI develops and distributes a security management process, security practices, and an information security evaluation method to enable organizations to protect their systems against current and emerging threats.

The Networked Systems Survivability technical program consists of the following projects:

- CERT Coordination Center

- Survivable Network Management

- Survivable Network Technology

- Extranet for Security Professionals (ESP)

CERT Coordination Center

Described on the CERT Web site, the CERT Coordination Center team provides technical assistance to system administrators who:

- Are on a networked host, and have the practical responsibility for the security of their site's computing systems.

- Would like to share information with colleagues at other sites.

- Could use technical and administrative recommendations to advance their system security.

- Want to take advantage of fixes to enhance the security of products on which they rely.

- Are facing a computer security emergency.

- Need help with a security breach that has already happened.

The center has experts on call for emergencies (widespread denial-of-service attacks, orchestrated attacks on Internet sites, etc.) 24 hours a day. The CERT Coordination Center:

• Is a 24-hour single point of contact for emergencies.

• Has the capability to facilitate communications among experts working to solve problems.

• Is a central point for the identification and correction of security vulnerabilities.

• Is a secure repository of computer security incident information.

Suggested Readings

The following list of books is offered to help you add to your library on Internet privacy—which no single book alone could possibly cover. Book descriptions and editorial reviews were culled from a variety of sources, including jacket covers, book reviews, publisher reviews, and our own reviews.

Database Nation: The Death of Privacy in the
21st Century
by Simson Garfinkel
O'Reilly & Associates; ISBN: 1565926536

Fifty years ago, in *1984*, George Orwell imagined a future in which privacy was decimated by a totalitarian state that used spies, video surveillance, historical revisionism, and control over the media to maintain its power. Those who worry about personal privacy and identity—especially in this day of technologies that encroach upon these rights—still use Orwell's Big Brother language to discuss privacy issues. But the reality is that the age of a monolithic Big Brother is over. And yet the threats are perhaps even more likely to destroy the rights we've assumed were ours. Today's threats to privacy are more widely distributed than they were in Orwell's state, and they represent both public and private interests. Over the next 50 years, we'll see new kinds of threats to privacy that don't find their roots in totalitarianism but in capitalism, the free market, advances in technology, and the unbridled exchange of electronic information.

The Electronic Privacy Papers: Documents on the Battle for Privacy in the Age of Surveillance
by Bruce Schneier, David Banisar
John Wiley & Sons; ISBN: 0471122971

While most books on privacy and security issues in cyberspace simply give accounts of debates on the issues, *The Electronic Privacy Papers* documents the war—practically salvo by salvo. Authors Schneier and Banisar present the actual government and industry documents, which cover both legal and technical matters. This book will give you a clear understanding of both sides of the debate and will provide insight into the strategies that both government and privacy advocates use in an attempt to achieve their desired result.

The Hundredth Window: Protecting Your Privacy and Security in the Age of the Internet
by Charles Jennings, Lori Fena, Esther Dyson
Free Press; ISBN: 068483944X

Privacy, whether we like it or not, has gone public. We are only just beginning to recognize how the Internet has redefined the relationship between our private lives and the public sphere. Every time we personalize a Web site, join a mailing list, or purchase a book or CD online, we open our lives to an ever-widening data network that offers us scant protection from the prying eyes of corporations, governments, insurance companies, or criminals. Has the e-commerce revolution permanently eroded all personal boundaries, or is it still possible to protect one's personal information in an increasingly wired world?

Charles Jennings and Lori Fena have devoted their careers to this question, most notably as the founders of TRUSTe. They have been instrumental in developing standards for judging how Web sites use and protect the personal information they collect, and they have advised numerous corporations that recognize that trust is the key to economic growth and expansion in the e-commerce world.

I Love the Internet, But I Want My Privacy, Too!
by Chris Peterson
Prima Publishing; ISBN: 0761514368

Chris Peterson has created a highly pragmatic guide for all those who want to enjoy the benefits of the Internet but are concerned about maintaining their privacy. Peterson examines the trade-offs, showing how properly shared information can provide you with important services, from enhancing your health care to protecting you from criminal activity. The flip side, however, is that erroneous information can prevent you from finding employment, deny you credit, or even bring you into conflict with law enforcement.

Peterson also shows how to watch for online scams and how to deal with the possibility of erroneous information. Several times throughout the book she pauses for a "privacy profile exercise," to help you discover what information about yourself is already public on the Internet or what information is being exchanged between your computer and others to keep track of your online activities.

Life and Death on the Internet
by Keith A. Schroeder (Editor), Julie Ledger
Supple Publishing; ISBN: 0966644204

Life and Death on the Internet is not only a must for parents; businesses need this book, too. With liability risks lurking around every corner in the business world you must keep employees from infecting your computer system with illegal material. Pornography acquired or brought to work could result in a sexual harassment lawsuit.

None of Your Business: World Data Flows, Electronic Commerce, & the European Privacy Directive
by Peter P. Swire, Robert E. Litan
Brookings Institute; ISBN: 081578239X

The historic European Union Directive on Data Protection took effect in October 1998. A key provision will prohibit transfer of personal information from Europe to other countries if they lack "adequate" protection of privacy. If enforced as written, the directive could create enormous obstacles to commerce between Europe and other countries, such as the United States, that do not have comprehensive privacy statutes. In this book, Swire and Litan provide the first detailed analysis of the sector-by-sector effects of the directive. They examine such topics as the text of the directive, the tension between privacy laws and modern information technologies, issues affecting a wide range of businesses and other organizations, effects on the financial services sector, and effects on other prominent sectors with large transborder data flows. In light of the many and significant effects of the directive

as written, the book concludes with detailed policy recommendations on how to avoid a coming trade war with Europe.

The Privacy Rights Handbook: How to Take
Control of Your Personal Information
by Privacy Rights Clearinghouse, Dale Fetherling (editor)
Avon Books (Pap Trd); ISBN: 0380786842

Your business has become big business. In our technologi-
cally advanced world, sensitive information about you—from
your medical history to your net worth—can be collected without
your knowledge and sold to the highest bidder; this information
may have been taken from records without your permission, or
you may have unwittingly revealed it yourself in the course of a
normal day. The good news is that you can fight back.

Beth Givens, founder of the Privacy Rights Clearinghouse,
gives you all the information you need to be aware of threats to
your privacy and to be assertive about protecting it. Find out why
your social security number is more revealing than you think, how
toll-free numbers and supermarket scanners can keep tabs on you,
what your employer can learn about you through your computer,
how much the government knows about you, and much more.

Protect Your Privacy on the Internet
by Bryan Pfaffenberger
John Wiley & Sons; ISBN: 0471181439

Get the strategies and software you need to protect your privacy on the Net. As more and more business is conducted over the
Internet, it has become increasingly difficult for both businesses
and individual users to protect private information. Your reputation, your finances, and your basic right to privacy are on the line
every day. What can you do about it?

You can fight back. *Protect Your Privacy on the Internet* tells you everything you need to know to ensure your privacy and use the same technology that's being used against you to protect yourself. You'll also get industrial-strength encryption tools to keep your affairs secret that the way they ought to be.

Public Policy and the Internet: Privacy, Taxes,
and Contract
by Nicholas Imparato (Editor)
Hoover Inst Press; ISBN: 0817998926

In October 1999, a group of prominent executives, Hoover fellows, and academics met to discuss Internet public policy, focusing initially on privacy and taxation but then expanding the debate to include issues of contract and jurisdiction as well. *Public Policy and the Internet* presents the initial findings that framed those discussions and outlines proposals that should guide policy-making in the future.

Security and Privacy for E-Business
by Anup K. Ghosh
John Wiley & Sons; ISBN: 0471384216

An in-depth look at the pressing issues involved in protecting an e-business from external threats while safeguarding customer privacy. This book examines the external threats to a company's system and explains how to react if your system and business goals diverge. It also presents a nuts-and-bolts guide to enhancing security and safeguarding gateways. Readers will find an extensive reference section for the many tools, standards, and watchdog agencies that aid in the security/privacy effort.

Technology and Privacy: The New Landscape
by Philip E. Agre (Editor), Marc Rotenberg (Editor)
MIT Press; ISBN: 0262511010

This book is a series of ten scholarly essays that lay a foundation for understanding the current state of technology-based privacy issues. The diverse group of contributors encompasses the fields of communications, human-computer interaction, law, political science, and sociology. Each contributor provides a capsule view of a privacy concern with an eye toward where things now stand and what bodes for the future. The book's most prevalent theme focuses on how advances in cybertechnology have led to greater threats to personal privacy, but have also led to greater promise for privacy protection.

Who Knows: Safeguarding Your Privacy in a Networked World
by Ann Cavoukian, Don Tapscott (contributor)
McGraw-Hill; ISBN: 0070633207

This is a scary but very necessary look at how "privacy" is fast becoming a quaint notion in today's wired world. Medical records, credit reports, employment records, and communications—a huge amount of information is profiled and stored online, very detailed, and often for sale. Everyday transactions such as buying a car, purchasing groceries, and ordering a pizza for delivery all seem innocuous, but information is collected about our preferences and habits in places that we don't usually consider. The authors show how information is amassed and maintained and then offer strategies and ideas for keeping the promise of technology from becoming a nightmare.

Glossary of
E-Privacy Terms

The following glossary of privacy terms come from a variety of public Internet sources, including TRUSTe, IDcide, and terms found throughout the book.

Access: This is a privacy requirement—one of the Fair Information Practices. Individuals should be able to find out what information is in their files and how the information is being used. Individuals must be able to correct information in their records.

Aggregate information: Information that may be collected by a Web site but is not "personally identifiable" to you. Aggregate information includes demographic data, domain names, Internet provider addresses, and Web site traffic. As long as none of these fields is linked to a user's personal information, the data are considered aggregate.

Browser cache: A memory file in your Web browser that stores the Internet addresses of sites you've recently visited. This capability allows you to access sites quicker.

Bulletin board: A public area online where you can post a message for everyone else to read. If you post a message to a bulletin board, in nearly all cases, other member participants will be able to contact you by e-mail.

Chat: A function that allows a group of people to communicate simultaneously by typing messages to one another online. Typically, everyone participating in the chat sees your message as soon as you send it. Designated chat areas are often referred to as "chat rooms," and any individual or group of individuals you respond to in the room will be able to contact you by e-mail.

Chief Privacy Officer (CPO): The official who is charged with ensuring that his or her organization develops and sticks to a privacy policy. The position often entails communicating with and instructing all employees and managers who have access to and responsibility for the organization's online infrastructure.

Children's Online Privacy Protection Act: Also referred to as COPPA. Often considered the first widespread government regulation of privacy on the Internet, this act went into effect on 21 April 2000. COPPA sets restrictions for Web sites that communicate with children under thirteen. One of these restrictions mandates that Web sites obtain "verifiable parental consent" before engaging in ongoing communications with a child.

Click Stream: A record of all the Web page addresses you have visited during a specific online session. Click trails tell not just what Web site you visited, but which pages inside that site.

Consent: This is a privacy requirement—one of the Fair Information Practices. People must be able to prevent the collection of their personal data. If they consent to use of their data, they should be able to bar the use of it for other than the original purpose.

Cookies: Cookies are small text files that Web sites place in your computer to help your browsers remember specific information. They are also used to store your preferences for content or personalized pages. Most shopping cart programs use cookies as well. These allow you to choose items and leave the virtual store, then return later and find that all the items are still in your shopping cart. Cookies are also used to build a profile of which sites you visit and which banner ads you click on. Advertisers use this information to deliver targeted ads directly to your computer. Some sites save your preferences on the cookie itself. Other sites assign users ID numbers or encoded passwords and keep records of your preferences at their end. Some sites use temporary cookies (called session cookies) that are deleted when you exit your browser. Others place persistent cookies, which stay on your hard drive for long periods.

The Code of Fair Information Practices: Basic principles defining proper handling of personal information. See the specific definitions for key requirements, including Notice, Consent, Access, and Security.

Collaborative filtering: A means of predicting the interests and needs of a specific customer based on previously collected data from a larger group of customers.

Domain name: The company, individual, or organization "name" you use to access a Web site, e.g. www.xyzco.org.

Electronic mail: Commonly referred to as e-mail, this form of communication enables you to send messages and files from your computer through an online service or the Internet to one or more e-mail addresses.

E-mail: See electronic mail.

E-mail address: The computer version of a postal address. Like a postal address, it contains information about who the e-mail recipient is and where he or she resides on the Internet.

Encryption: Data that is scrambled into a private code for secure transmission.

Forms: Any document that contains blank fields that surfers can fill in with data. The fields may contain any personal information, such as name, address, e-mail address, phone number, etc. A form is the most common and easiest tool used to collect information.

Identity theft: The use of personal information to falsely assume your identity.

Infomediaries: Persons or organizations that specialize in personal information management for individual Internet users.

Internet access provider: See Internet service provider.

Internet service provider (ISP): Also called an Internet access provider. A company that provides direct access to the Internet for individuals, companies, and institutions. Unlike commercial online service providers, ISPs usually do not provide their own content but may offer e-mail capability, browser software, and direct links to sites on the World Wide Web.

Newsgroup: Topic groupings for articles and information posted by readers of that group. If you post a message to a newsgroup, other participants of the group will know your e-mail address.

Notice: This is a privacy requirement—one of the Fair Information Practices. Web site users should be affirmatively and clearly told what information is collected about them and how it will be used.

Online service: A proprietary, commercial network that provides a variety of information and other services to its subscribers. Commercial online services typically provide their own content, forums (e.g. chat rooms, bulletin boards), e-mail capability, and information available only to subscribers.

Opt in: An option that gives you complete control over the collection and dissemination of your personal information. A site that provides this option is stating that it will not gather or track information about you unless you knowingly provide such information and consent to the site. The debate within the Internet arena asks whether people should be able to opt out (see opt out) of information collection by a site, as they do at most sites today;

or whether they should affirmatively opt in—requiring each site to ask each user whether he or she wants to be a part of its data-collection effort.

Opt out: An option that gives you the choice to prevent personally identifiable information from being used by a particular Web site or shared with third parties.

Password: A private, unique series of letters and/or numbers that you create and must use to gain access to an online service or the Internet, specific data available online, or to make modifications to restricted-access software (e.g., parental control software).

Personally identifiable information: Information that can be traced back to an individual user (e.g., your name, postal address, or e-mail address). Personal user preferences tracked by a Web site via a cookie (see definition above) is also considered personally identifiable when linked to other personally identifiable information provided by you online.

Privacy enhancing technologies: Software, tools, and related policies that work to safeguard your online privacy and security. See P3P.

Privacy seal: Also referred to as a trustmark. An online seal awarded to Web sites that agree to post their privacy practices openly via privacy statements, as well as to adhere to enforcement procedures that ensure that their privacy promises are met. See trustmark.

Privacy statement or privacy policy: A page or pages on a Web site that lay out its privacy policies (i.e., what personal information is collected by the site, how it will be used, whom it will be shared with, and whether you have the option to exercise control over how your information will be used).

P3P: The Platform for Privacy Preferences Project (P3P) is an emerging standard that enables Web sites to state their privacy practices in a standard format that browser plug-ins can retrieve automatically and interpret easily. These plug-ins will enable users to be informed of site practices (in both machine- and human-readable formats) and to automate decision-making based on these practices when appropriate. Thus users need not read the privacy policies at every site they visit.

Privacy policy or privacy statement: An organization's statement explaining what personal data, if any, it collects about its users and how it uses that information. It's a binding contract between an organization and its visitors and users.

Referrer field: The referrer header field (mistakenly spelled "referer" in the HTTP standard) is a unit of information that contains the URL of the site you are currently in. The referrer header field is sent automatically to any site you are about to visit, when clicking a link. Referrer headers allow reading patterns to be studied and reverse links drawn. The address of the page might contain privacy information (such as your name or e-mail address), or might reveal personal interests that you would rather keep private (e.g., http://www.examplesite.com/Health/Medicine/Dermatology/).

Seal programs: Independent programs that attempt to help Web sites deal better with privacy.

Security: This is a privacy requirement—one of the Fair Information Practices. Any organization creating, maintaining, using, or disseminating records of personally identifiable information must ensure the reliability of, and must take precautions to prevent misuse of, such information.

Spam: Also called junk e-mail. Unsolicited, unwanted e-mail usually sent by advertisers. Spam is usually sent out to thousands of unwilling recipients at once.

Spam filters: Programs that detect and reject spam by looking for certain keywords, phrases, or Internet addresses.

Third-party ad servers: Companies that display banner advertisements on Web sites that you visit. These companies are often not the ones that own the Web site.

Trustmark: An online seal awarded to Web sites that agree to post their privacy practices openly via privacy statements, as well as adhere to enforcement procedures that ensure that their privacy promises are kept.

Index